A Third Whe...

The Eccentric Alternative

A Guide to
Sidecars and Trikes

Simon Potter

Panther Publishing

Published by Panther Publishing Ltd in 2009
Panther Publishing Ltd
10 Lime Avenue
High Wycombe
Buckinghamshire HP11 1DP, UK
http://www.panther-publishing.com

Dedication

To my brother, Mike and wife, Mary - the first people to bike with me!

Acknowledgements
The bulk of the photographs are from the author's collection. The author is particularly grateful to Peter Rivers-Fletcher and Watsonian Squire Ltd, Martin Conquest Ltd, F2 Motorcycles, Wildcat Trikes, Colin Appleyard, Boom Trikes (UK), Merlin Sidecars, Trike Designs, and also to Roy Richards and the National Motorcycle Museum and to *Outlook,* the magazine of the Federation of Sidecar Clubs, for permission to use images from catalogues, photographs of motorcycles in their collection and magazine covers. The author apologises for those few images for which prior permission could not be obtained, although every effort has been made to find their source and seek permission. To the many individuals who were willing to let their pride and joy be photographed, and to those who could not be asked, the author's thanks are warmly extended.

ISBN 978-0-9556595-7-7

Contents

INTRODUCTION

Few, if any, motorcyclists leave the machine they buy as stock. If the bike is naked and retro-styled the number of accessories which can be permanently fitted is legion: screens, fairings, panniers, top-boxes, mud-flaps, luggage racks, steering dampers, new silencers - generally not to increase silence - crash bars and LED stop lights. Some of these help with touring, as do the further additions of larger fuel tanks, tank-top bags, drive-chain Scott-oilers, SATNAV, heated handle-bar grips, gel seats, foot-boards and back-supports. Some help the bike to go faster, such as changes to cams and carburettors, different air filters, oil coolers and radiators; some make the bike *look* as if they might make it go faster, like rear-set foot-pegs and clip-on bars.

In the world of both the 'metric cruiser' and Harley-Davidson, there are hundreds of little bits that can be purchased, after poring over closely-packed pages of catalogues, such as chromed nut-covers, cable-supports, hidden cable-run bars, billet wheels, hub-caps, braided brake piping, extra running lights, white-wall tyres, fork shrouds, and different fenders, mirrors, indicators and saddles. All this may be done without actually commissioning someone else to customise your machine more radically.

This desire to customise is obviously part of the mind-set which leads someone to buy a motorbike in the first place - and the phenomenon is by no means new, as a glance over a page of accessories from a '60s magazine will show, although it has expanded exponentially with increased prosperity. It is clearly something to do with the desire for individuality, an urge towards non-conformity. Of course, a bike lends itself to the attachment of a myriad accessories in ways that a car doesn't quite manage to do. The skills, facilities and money required to make substantial (and legal) changes to bodywork and running-gear on a car are

'60s advertisements

Top left, 1950s Bond minicar. Top speed 40mph, less with four aboard. Trikes in post-war Britain tended to have roofs and to be strictly utilitarian.; they offered a perceptibly more civilised environment to a family man than a sidecar outfit - if with only a fraction of an outfit's performance.

Top Right, a 1960s plastic Bond minivan which used a Hillman Imp water-cooled engine giving far more oomph.

Left, what lay under the capacious bonnet of a Bond micro-car: a tiny Villiers air-cooled single, originally of 122cc. The first of these trikes were started using a cord starter. As a last resort they could be started by stepping into the open bonnet and jumping on the kick-starter. If you weren't careful, the bonnet would become un-propped and fall; the car then looked as if it was eating you.

Below, a 1930s trike. The Morgan with 1000cc Matchless V-twin power.

all of a high order, as the Custom and Classic car movement can attest. The ability to personalise and tweak a bike needs less space, less money and (in most cases) less specialised technical and engineering knowledge - and the manufacturers know this. Instant satisfaction is guaranteed when a louder exhaust can is fitted at no great cost and with an adjustable spanner in the roadway in front of the house.

Yet there is one accessory, the ultimate accessory in terms of the changes it brings to both the life of its buyer and to the use and performance of the bike to which it is fitted, and that is the addition of a third wheel. Going for a sidecar, or, in a parallel conversion to three wheels, for a trike, is to make a very great difference to your experience as a motorcyclist. Shoving a go-faster can, some LEDs or a fly-screen on your bike won't change your life, nor the way in which you are perceived by others; converting it into a sidecar outfit or motor-tricycle most definitely will.

Why would anyone want to turn a bicycle into a tricycle? When, between 1920 and 1960, the cost and limited availability of motorcars of any sort put them outside the scope of all but the rich, one answer to that question was to carry the tools of a trade and transport wife and children. In the post WWII era it is safe to assume that almost all keen young motorcyclists had to bolt a child/adult sidecar on eventually, or give up the bike. Another answer was, in the 1970s in the UK, to enable a novice rider to use a 650cc or even 1000cc bike with L-plates; without a 'chair' the rider was limited to 250cc. Some of the bikes of this 'classic' era between the last war and the decimation of the UK's motorcycle industry made adequate sidecar machines, but many didn't. Lack of oil-bath clutches and decent clutch material, the poor drum brakes, unsophisticated suspension, small lubrication reservoirs, weak frames and lower power of most machines, exacerbated by primitive contact breaker/magneto/6 volt electrical systems, meant that sidecar haulage was a high maintenance, low satisfaction business - even at the best of times.

The option of having a trike and driving it on a motorcycle licence meant buying, in the UK at least, one of a dozen quirky micro-cars, most powered by two-stroke engines of less than 250cc. The Bond, the Heinkel, the Trojan, the BMW Isetta, the Messerschmitt, the Peel, the Berkeley and the astonishing door-less Gordon (with its engine bolted on the side driving one wheel by chain) were all compromises dictated by cash considerations. Only Reliant with its Austin 7-derived, water-cooled 4 cylinder was a better bet - but it was nearly as expensive as a 'real' car.

Today, no such considerations exist. You buy a chair or trike nowadays because you *want* to. You've got a car - well, so have tens of millions of others - but you want what only a motorcycle with sidecar or a finely-made powered tricycle can give: a challenge and a conversation-piece. You may have grown prudent with advancing wisdom and realised that an outfit or a trike is a much safer way to continue biking. You may intend that your machine be of real use and you will use it every day for the open air it gives and the sheer fun of it, or you may slide it out of the driveway only on fine Sundays. You may want to preserve a little something of life in the '60s and run a classic bike with period sidecar, or you may feel that for maximum stimulation you need a long-legged tourer trike or outfit with the space and stamina to take you over the Alps and far away.

These are the types of 'you' at whom this little book is aimed - not exclusively at an oil-soaked, Barbour-clad, craggy-faced veteran of a thousand thunderstorms with no car licence and sidecar memories stretching back before the Beatles (although such enthusiasts are not ruled out, of course); nor at a wheelie-pulling, tri-coloured leather-wearing, super-sports bike track-day aficionado (although he or she could sometime consider a totally different sort

4

B.S.A. MOTOR CYCLES LTD.
ARMOURY ROAD, BIRMINGHAM B11 2PX

Telephone: 021 - 772 2381
SERVICE DEPT. 021 - 772 2381

YOUR REF.

OUR REF.   SERV/AJH/GH

TELEGRAMS AND CABLES
"SELMOTO, BIRMINGHAM"
TELEX : 33315

31st. July 1972.

Mr. S.C. Potter,
Appartment 8,
Via. Forini 12,
Montecatini Terme,
Italy.

Dear Sir,

We thank you for your recent letter, and are pleased to learn of your obvious satisfaction with your Bantam B175 machine.

Quite frankly, we do not consider that this type of machine is suitable for sidecar work, although we understand that certain private owners have carried out such an attachment previously. As far as we are aware, practically the only sidecar makers still in being in this country is Messrs. Watsonian of Greet, Birmingham.11. We would suggest that you write to them in this connection, concerning a suitable sidecar, possibly of fibreglass type.

If you go ahead with your idea, it will be necessary for you to find a way of reducing the overall gear ratios, possibly by fitting a smaller than standard gearbox sprocket, and a larger than standard rear chainwheel.

Yours faithfully
B.S.A. MOTORCYCLES LIMITED.

A.J. HARPER.
SERVICE DEPARTMENT.

of biking culture), but at that new you – the one who will experience the greatest satisfaction possible on any road vehicle when you are piloting a wayward, improbable machine over which you must have complete control at all times and aboard which you will eventually feel impregnably safe and will forget everything except the coordinating joys of mastery.

Why the improbable has happened, and sidecars and trikes continue to exist

Piloting an outfit and feeling the whole device rolling beneath you is a hard-to-explain sensation, which only a small number of bikers know about. It may alone explain the continuing phenomenon of the sidecar combination. I know that I never seem to possess a bike for more than a year or two (generally until the manufacturer's warranty, with its usual discouragement of sidecar fitment, has run out) without getting a new chair fitted to it. This has been a *leitmotif* of my motorcycling since 1971 when I wrote to what remained of BSA asking if it would be possible to fit a light sidecar to the 175cc Bantam I then rode. They were not enthusiastic, rightly I now realise. Watsonian, the famous sidecar manufacturers were more encouraging, suggesting a pilgrimage to Munday's of Brixton, London. What I bought from them - a bright blue Ural M66 with sidecar - exchanging the little Bantam to do it, kicked-off my involvement with outfits. Now I experience a leap of attention whenever I see a combo - rather like that expansion of consciousness felt when one realises one has heard thunder, not just an aircraft. I've an almost as close affinity with trikes; they too inhabit a fascination zone shared with valve hi-fi and steam and diesel railroad locos.

It is anachrophilia which has spawned the brotherhood of readers of all those classic bike, commercial classic truck, car and railway magazines which rise, brightly seductive, from floor to eye-level in newsagents all over the western world. Each promises a quick fix for the mildly agreeable illness of *nostalgie*. Of course, the malady is not treated by such purchases, any more than it is cured by visits to bike shows, preserved railways, swap-meets and auto-jumbles; nor by the arrival of membership gazettes from the many clubs to which someone with these interests can belong. Rather, these prophylactics serve only to increase the itch.

I believe that our fascination with such things is the product of a frustrated desire to possess a hands-on grasp of how things work, of the maintenance of a 1960s/70s world of early adulthood and of a fondness for things manufactured in the homeland. For these reasons it is rare to see very young people writing, reading or purchasing in this field.

The theory that we are somehow made uneasy when we cannot grasp how our technology works is a pessimistic one. In early medieval times every single person in a community, except perhaps the village idiot, would have been able to grasp how a wheelbarrow was made and how it worked. Most important, anyone could have made a wheelbarrow for himself. By the late middle-ages there must have been quite a lot of people who had no idea how an abbey *horloge* worked, let alone would have been able to design the clock mechanism from scratch. In Shakespeare's plays the presence of maps and letters nearly always spelt disaster, (do you remember the story lines of *King Lear* and *Romeo and Juliet*?) In an age when only a few Dutch and English cartographers could

Right, early post-war Panther M100 600cc single on Steib chair. Some find the chunky appeal of bolts, nuts, rods and easily understood mechanics of a classic outfit like this irresistible. Notice the girder forks, considered better for sidecar work than the contemporary skinny telescopic forks on offer, and the fact that the engine, which acts as a stressed frame member on a Panther 100, is used as a mounting point for the lower front sidecar strut.

Below, really big boys Meccano - a staggering V8 trike with all the working bits on view. Mind you, to be really practical it needs mudguards on those big rear wheels.

make maps and less than one per-cent of the population could read, such sinister mysteries were regarded rather as computers were later to be regarded in *A Space Odyssey* or *Jurassic Park* - as having the potential for human vice or ill luck to bring about tragedy.

From the Renaissance onwards the process accelerated: the secrets of how to make atmospheric engines were confined to a tiny few in the late 18th century; fewer still could make or understand high-pressure steam engines or electric motors sixty years later. By the time radio, radar, nuclear fission, micro-chips and genetic engineering became commonplace – at least as far as misgivings about application were concerned, if not intellectual ownership by the general populace - the grasp of the ordinary person was lost.

There is a big gap between owning and using something and understanding and being able to replicate it. Even that humblest of modern miracles, the ball-point pen, is way beyond the ability of any individual person to manufacture at home from scratch. Between wheelbarrow and biro 'there is a great gulf fixed'.

The sense that the drift of the future and the control of technology lies in a few hands ('them') is bound to be unsettling to those who have no *entrée* into the secrets - that is to say 'us'. This is what lies behind the conspiratorial apocalypticism of the post-Cold War world. And it is no doubt why a fascination with and a love of technologies from fifty to a hundred years ago is so prevalent in a certain age group. This cannot be entirely new: from the refusal of the Provost of Eton College, England to allow the Great Western Railway to build a station near the school to the diehard devotion to the horse and carriage in the early days of the automobile and 'stink-bike', the cry of the middle-aged seems to have been: 'put the clock back to simpler, better days'.

Now, in the 21st century, we are in a slightly different position. The speed-up of technological advances in electronics has made it impossible for even the above-average enthusiast to keep up, so a ready acceptance of change and of modernity is matched with the desire to acquire new things, especially among the young. Also, the various threats to the survival of mankind are now accepted as being likely to be *averted*, rather than caused, by the pursuit of scientific advance. This is no doubt why almost all devotees of simple technology seem to be over fifty; they were brought up in the *Doctor Strangelove* era of cold war to fear such advance.

So, in a particular stratum of the population, there is that feeling that a world of Eastman colour, Meccano, Lionel Trains and Ovaltine is not absolutely lost just yet - must not be lost, because in that world, for the last time, a certain post-war generation actually understood how things worked. And that's where such things as sidecars and trikes fit in, I feel.

Motorcycles and sidecars are joined together by chunky steel nuts and bolts, by lengths of tough tubing. Adjustments to get the whole ensemble to run sweetly are made with spanners, soft-headed hammers, straight edges of wood, plumb lines and, above all, eye and feel. Electrical connections are no more complex than wiring up the speakers to your hi-fi of the 1960s; dampers and swivelling joints need oil and grease. It is all so Meccano, so rooted in the comprehensible and real.

Not just challenging, unknown and expensive, but characterful enough to be odd!

I wasn't sure what to subhead this little book. 'The Challenging Alternative' seemed right because of the changes to driving and lifestyle owning an outfit or trike brings about, but a motorcycling friend suggested 'The Ultimate Accessory' when he learned that an indulgence in a third wheel can take three or four months to manufacture and might dispose of £10,000 ($15,000). Then I felt that 'The Invisible Alternative' might hit the nail more accurately because, although there are currently 6 providers of sidecars in the UK and they always say they are rushed off their feet by demand, you never see one on the roads. From Ramsgate to Plymouth, from Eastbourne to Oban, you can drive on every type of road and not spot a combination (or trike), except by the merest chance. When you know that there are 12 expensive manufacturers and importers of sidecars in North America alone, but that you can travel from Seattle to Savannah, Halifax N.S. to Regina and never spot one, you begin to realise how apt the moniker 'Invisible Alternative' actually is. But finally I settled on 'The Eccentric Alternative' - it seems to say it all!

There are famous manufacturers in Switzerland, Germany and Holland, and it is true that I have clocked more than one motorcycle combo in the same day in those countries, but Great Britain is sometimes called 'the home of the sidecar' - after all, the Graham Brothers 1903 Liberty Sociable Side-carriage originated here - yet the roads seem empty of them.

This is why, when you have taken your treasured bike to one of those manufacturers and said: "Go ahead!", you have set out upon a momentous journey. You have done more than place a bit of metal and plastic alongside your steed, you have entered another cosmos. In this alternative world there is no point in wishing to go un-remarked. At every traffic light, old guys will smile or leap with recognition, children will stare, sometimes calling out: "Wow!" or "Nice One!" or "Is that the Batbike?" and, when parked, conversations will ensue. However modern your bike is, your interlocutors will initially

A rare modern sight: a combination on a British motorway - in this case a Ural, looking rather stately on its 19" wheels and moving with calm purpose at about 55mph towards the West Country.

think you are riding something from the '50s or '60s, and they always think your sidecar is ancient, but beautifully preserved, and they express amazement when you tell them it was manufactured last month.

Then there is the reaction of other road users. Generally your previously easily-missed bike is now highly visible, so you suffer no more from the hasty puller-out who 'didn't see you'. Generally too, automobile drivers are not as impatient as they might be if you were proceeding as slowly in a car. They automatically assume that a combo is going to slow them up, as would a tractor or road-roller. It's often a surprise to them how quickly an outfit can be made to move, if the mood takes you. Their assumptions do mean, though, that they can't bear to let you stay ahead of them for long - and you need to prepare for this. I suppose it's just that, for once, they can get round a motorcyclist instead of him or her getting round them. There is still a widespread notion, I'm sure, among people of a certain vintage, that a sidecar outfit is an inferior mode of transport; that you *would* have a car if, poor sap, you could afford it. This is the other psycho-social reason for their wanting to be ahead of you, not behind you. You must not mind this. On country roads, when you are enjoying the calm charms of an outfit being driven moderately, you must be prepared to pull over sometimes and let the impatient ones past. I didn't do this on one occasion when carefully running-in an outfit through roads in the plastic countryside surrounding London. Mr Nasty of Surrey got so angry at being held up for a few precious moments that he pulled alongside and screamed: "You bastard! I hope you have a crash and die!" This has, however, been the only unpleasing moment in over 35 years of running combos, so I can vouch for it being atypical.

That quiet, insistent inner voice asking: "Is it safe?"

In practice what others think doesn't matter and shouldn't ruffle your well-being. A lot more important is the consideration of safety. On a solo you do feel vulnerable. Like Ishmael, your hand is against all men's and theirs is against yours. On a combination you are not trying all the time to balance, of course, and this makes a *huge* difference. A boy once asked me, as I manoeuvred past him solo on a big Jap cruiser, "How *can* you balance something so heavy? Why doesn't it fall over?" Balancing these large machines of 300kg or more is a surprising trick when you let your mind focus on it. I have felt suddenly very uneasy travelling near the edge of a motorway flyover, or moving between two rows of thundering trucks, as I have unexpectedly questioned exactly what I am doing. And to question it brings that worrying insecurity - a kind of ebb of confidence. Maynard Hershon wrote once in *Motorcycle Sport and Leisure* of the two or three occasions when, without warning, he fell off his bike. At the time he wondered if there was a problem with his nervous system, with his ability to continue doing the seemingly impossible. Riding a pushbike down a grassy track is one thing; holding course on a GoldWing at 60mph between lines of highway traffic is another. Last summer I saw a notice on the back of a trike at Box Hill, Surrey, an English bikers' gathering place. It read 'Whatever you think of this trike, remember this: it cannot fall over' .

At the back of one's mind, as one is whizzing along on a solo, is always that whispering voice: "Okay, so what happens if I get a blow-out/my transmission jams/a dog runs out *now?*" Also present, on the horizon of the mind, are the casualty figures - especially those uncomfortable ones about the highest biker death-rates being among the 45-55 year olds with slowing reflexes. Somehow piloting a sidecar outfit removes all these subliminal fears. You do feel very safe; in rain, in snow, on fallen leaves, in frost, over diesel spills and - an additional pleasure - on sunny days when you can ride un-gloved in a T-shirt and not risk the horrors of road-burn should the worst happen. You have the higher eye-position that a motorcycle affords over a car, and you have virtual 200 degree vision. Your machine does not wobble or wander if you turn round, as a solo can do.

Obviously, that old 1950s saw about a combination being 'the safest vehicle on the road' really isn't true. Whatever you may *feel* about being on your outfit or trike, you

Another way of making a Dragstar 1100 stable. One of the author's bikes in the snow, attached to a Unit Hedingham Sprite sidecar. You don't have a second's qualm in icy conditions on a combo because of the single wheel drive.

don't have a metal shell around you, nor seat-belts, nor air-bags. But the thing that makes the most difference is that you just give up taking risks when you have fitted a chair or got triked.

I have always found - and talking to other motorcyclists confirms this - that when I ride a solo machine I tend to shave seconds off journeys more and more often - just because I can do so. I have often found myself travelling quickly between rows of traffic, or zapping along outside that stationary jam (when entitled to do so in Europe and those US states that permit it) faster than the recommended 5 - 10mph more than the line being passed. More than once someone fed up with being stuck has decided to try another

This machine won't fall over! A Yamaha Dragstar 1100 converted to a trike. Note the lengthened front fork stanchions to lift this already imposing machine further off the ground.

route and has pulled out directly in front of me to make a U-turn. Every time it happens, every time I have that near miss, I swear that I will give up queue-jumping except where it is very safe and I will be going very, very slowly. But a week later, the narrow escape having faded in the memory, I'm at it again. Sometimes this rushing saves only three or four minutes at a slow junction - and those ridiculous few minutes seem to matter.

My father, Major W R Potter, was, for a time, quite well-known back in 1950s England for his writing and broadcasting about what he called MSU, the Malady of Supposed Urgency. He had identified half a century ago what nowadays we would more snappily term 'hurry sickness' - but it's the same thing. MSU is the solo motorcyclist's greatest enemy. And it doesn't matter how much you fight against the illogicality of taking big risks to save tiny amounts of time, you *always* do it again. It is utterly impossible to sit quietly behind other cars in a queue on a solo bike. The fact that other bikers are zipping past you makes what you are doing seem odd, and so you find yourself pulling out and taking those risks again - compelled, perhaps, only by a desire for conformity with your brother biker. In addition to this desire not to seem quaintly timorous, there is, in so many of us, a competitive urge that encourages us at least to try to keep up with other motorcyclists. This is more than ever the case now that small motorbikes like the BSA 'Bantam' or the other slow, workaday two-strokes of forty years ago from Francis-Barnett, James or Norman are never seen. Apart from Honda pizza delivery bikes and the urban scooter, the majority of machines on the roads are big sports replicas, tourers or cruisers - and it would seem ridiculous to poodle along in the gutter on any of these. MSU's dangers are not confined to motorcyclists, of course. Everyone is in a hurry, not just to get close to you, or past you, but actually to possess the space that you occupy. Such is the effect of crowded roads, and it does put off many a would-be motorcyclist who is not made of gladiatorial (or suicidal) material.

Driving a combination or trike is already a statement of non-conformity, as I have suggested, so you are immediately excused from doing what the solo rider more or less *has* to do. It's surprisingly peaceful to be both on a motorcycle and not rushing anywhere - a best of both worlds, rather than the worst of both. I have certainly relished the calming nature of piloting an outfit in London traffic, getting interest not from high-risk spurts of speed and dodging, but from finding arcane rat-runs down quiet, narrow roads; the point being to keep moving, rather than to save time. In this way, the journey becomes a pleasure - neither distracted by radio or CD in a metal box, nor disturbed by the sub-knowledge of risk-taking.

The sidecar outfit or bike-based trike conversion is, generally, small enough and lithe enough to escape from the worst of snarl-ups, and I have sometimes put the third

NORTON 250 Jubilee Twin

FRANCIS BARNETT
250 Cruiser Twin

JAMES 200 Sports Captain

Left, market leading British bikes of 45 or more years ago - all from Assoiciated Motorcycles, and all designed for the top end of the learner market. By comparison with these, a 650cc sports combo seemed pretty fast!

Right, combinations can take liberties which cars can't. Put a car where this outfit is in central London and the police or a traffic warden would appear in seconds. Sidecars can also use bike parking spaces, are exempt from the London congestion charge and , when occasion demands, are able to filter past stationary traffic like a solo or take short cuts over pavements. Not to be encouraged, of course, but a reminder that they can be lithe and flexible - provided their track is not too enormous of course. About 48 inches is ideal.

wheel on the pavement to reach a turning, got between bollards to access a quieter street, or done a U-turn within my own length to seek a new path in a manner which even a Smart car or Mini can't manage.

It is in poor weather that the peculiar joys of a three-wheeler come into their own. When a strong side-wind is buffeting across the lanes of the freeway, or a driving spring rain is sending up sprays of water from the passing cars and trucks, the sidecar combo or trike becomes a secure, tough little boat - like one of those buoyant lifeboats rising and falling with the breakers. As its pilot you are wet or wind-blown, but, in contrast with the fears which assail you on a solo machine, you remain somehow above it all. I have ridden in blinding snow and glassy frost and have never felt the slightest unease. Caught in a blizzard on a two-wheeler, you would be wise to park up and call a cab - but the combination, in particular, cannot skid; with a single wheel drive there is no other wheel to take the torque and start to spin uncontrollably. This is why limited slip differentials are so often specified for trikes. Just as a three-legged stool always has its feet firmly planted, however uneven the terrain, so does the three-wheeled vehicle. You sit, swaying with the suspension, feet firmly in place, lashed by water, snow or gale, and somehow *liking* it; you are back to nature, on your trusty horse or aboard that sturdy boat, but not in any danger.

It's an interesting mixture of dare and coddling, but (unlike some theme-park ride) on a machine over which you have complete control. More than a man upon a horse, you *are* the man/horse, for there is only one controlling intellect on a motorcycle. Man and his machine are in conjoined stasis, the machine extending and stabilizing the biped skeleton. The critic Hugh Kenner (although not writing about motorcycling!) thought of 'Man in Excelsis' as body and mind in closest harmony: 'the mind set on survival, mastery and the contemplation of unchanging relativities; the body a reduction to uncluttered, quintessential machine' - the philosopher Descartes' ideal marriage of mechanical mathematics and conscious absorption of information from it. But you do not suffer the outrageous weaknesses of joints, ageing limbs and improbable physics of movement which cruelly encumber the conscious biped - and, by extension, the pedalled bicycle. Upon a powered bicycle your direction of the machine is bedevilled by high centre of gravity, balance and fear. As part of a sidecar combo or trike you achieve perfect union with the machine; you are the 'Cartesian centaur' - half man, half machine.

Cartesian centaur - a Honda Valkyrie and well preserved Swallow single-seat sidecar

WHAT BIKE FOR YOUR CHAIR?

David Minton pointed out in his *Motorcyclists's Handbook* of 1981 that 'despite some claims to the contrary, all orthodox motorcycles can be fitted with sidecars providing it is correctly done. A well-fitted sidecar will strengthen, not weaken, a motorcycle frame.' Similarly, any sidecar can be attached to any bike. However, their marriage can be a fraught one if their compatibility is not thought about. There are various avenues into this matter of happy match-making: Does one want to carry a great deal? Go fast? Ride over rough ground? Create a combo which looks good? Create one which rides easily?

Many would-be combo riders have already owned their bike for some time, or so it has seemed to me when I've visited the workshops of British sidecar makers. I'm often rather interested to see how comparatively elderly and of low value some bikes are which are going to be allied to an expensive, colour-matched chair. Ten years or so doesn't

Top, Panther M120 650cc single with a Busmar Astral double-adult sidecar: just the sort of machine which families used in their thousands in the early sixties. These chairs can sometimes be found second-hand today from specialist firms like Charnwood Classic Restorations. They're an acquired taste, but fun.

Below, proof that a modern chair can grace an old bike. A Squire sports single-seater on a rare Scott water-cooled two-stroke twin

seem uncommon, but I guess a decent old machine which has been kept in good order and is running sweetly is as good a proposition as any for use as a sidecar tug. At least one hasn't the fear of damaging a brand-new bike, or, as I've mentioned before, running into warranty problems. Quite why the majority of bike firms discourage the fitting of a sidecar, I don't know. As the quotation above from David Minton has made clear, additional triangulation should give strength to a frame - especially those traditional cradle frames favoured by the V-twin cruisers and 'retro' street bikes which are popular among charioteers. While it is true that the task of haulage may put a little extra strain on wheel bearings, brake-pads, suspension units and clutch plates, these are disposable items which you would have thought the manufacturers would be pleased to have to sell as replacements every now and then.

The author's Yamaha Classic and Watsonian-Squire GP700 Jubilee, in this case the 650cc version of the bike. The 1100cc version with this chair is offered as a complete outfit by Watsonian Squire.

Below. Many European countries, including Britain, used simple, but rather fascinating three-wheelers in the post-war period of austerity. Here is a Motocart, immortalised for a particular generation by Dinky Toys' 1949 model, with its considerable bulk hauled by a diminutive air-cooled single, geared very low, driving the front wheel. The driver stood at the steering.

Some bikes nowadays seem to have no frames capable of taking clamps or welded lugs for a chair, but for these machines there are all sorts of sub-frames in existence. These locate to known strong points on the bike, such as engine mountings, and impose no greater strain on the bike's integrity than does a car's engine under its bonnet.

So the discouraging attitude of manufacturers - with the exceptions of Ural, Chang-Jiang, Royal Enfield and Moto Guzzi - means that it makes sense to let your bike's warranty run most of its cover before bolting on your chair. Interesting recent (2006 and 2007) exceptions to this are Watsonian-Squire's offering of a Yamaha XVS1100 'DragStar' Classic complete with GP Sports wide-body sidecar from new, and Unit Sidecars' Triumph triple complete with Hedingham sports chair from new. Yamaha, usually among the least encouraging of makers, does recognize this outfit for warranty purposes, and, as I know I'm not alone in thinking that the DragStar makes a very apt sidecar bike, you'd think they would relent on this model alone. Triumph, of course, were well-used to seeing their retro 'Thunderbird' triple on TV some years back carrying The Two Fat Ladies to their cooking assignments while hitched to a Watsonian GP wide body.

The engine capacity, power and torque of your chosen tractor all have their bearing on your choice of sidecar. After all, you will be involved in the creation of an outfit, a single unit, and the matching of the two components is a factor in the choice of both. In such a characterful area of road transport, there is a certain perverse pleasure, of course, in persevering with the mastery of two units which don't seem to match automatically. The two most obvious of these are the big, wide sidecar on a small, low-powered motorcycle and its complete converse. Each can make for extremely interesting driving, I have found, but the latter is ultimately a more lasting satisfaction.

Three eccentric Italian jobs - three combinations of engine capacity and gearing

Back in the early '70s, when I spent a lot of time in Tuscany, Italy, I was fascinated by three vehicles which I saw regularly. Although all were three-wheelers, only one was a sidecar outfit. The first was a quite large flat-bed lorry with very basic cab enclosing a handle-bar, forks, front-wheel, tank and saddle. Behind and under the cab was the tiniest 49cc two-stroke engine made, I think, by either Garelli or Minarelli, and driving the rear axle by means of an enormously long flapping chain. This was no compact 'Ape' from the Piaggio stable, but operated on the same lines. It was owned by a *contadino* friend of my mother's and I regularly spotted it climbing the fearful inclines to Borgo or Montecatini Alto with a vast tonnage of water-melons on board. Its driver crouched in the tinny cab, cap pulled over his eyes, and the truck screamed along at waking-pace with its enormous load, propelled by a piston not much bigger than a cotton-reel. The secret was, of course, in the gearing and it was an object lesson to me at the time that you did not necessarily need cubic centimetres. High revs and low, low speeds were quite acceptable. I believe that it was this device which gave me the confidence to think of fitting a chair to my Bantam. After all, *that* machine had a full 175ccs.

At the other end of the scale was the BSA 'sloper' which was harnessed to the largest side carriage I had ever seen - a mobile ice-cream parlour. As I lay awake in the hot dawn of Montecatini Terme, in my mother's flat on the western outskirts, up from Margine Coperta would come a steady, violent slamming - more of a bang than a thud - slow, even, barrel-chested. Lounging on the ancient sprung Lycett saddle, a one-armed war veteran with no larynx (when he spoke it sounded like the wind among the leaves) piloted his outrageously heavy outfit into Montecatini market. The sun did not reach him because he drove with two bright umbrellas up at each end of his square cream and chrome refrigerated side-box. Within its lined interior was hand-made ice-cream to last

Above, a Moto Guzzi Ercole 500cc horizontal single without a cab in its military incarnation. This tricycle is based on what, in a very different state of tune, became the Falcone - a famous sporty single. Below, the same trike with cab for civilian use. This enclosed version was hard work in Italian mid-summer temperatures.

This diesel Aermacchi commercial trike is quite sophisticated - it has a steering wheel.

all day: deep tubs of pistachio, banana, chocolate and *crema*. On the side-box top were rows of cones, spoons and glasses in racks. Drawers under the fridges were filled with crushed ice. He would park in exactly the same place each market day and perch on the BSA's saddle, serving ice-cream beneath his sun-shades. With the dusk came the deep, slow thud again, lighter by reason of going downhill with empty coolers.

This epic machine - almost certainly a WWII relic abandoned by the Allies, but since painted fire-engine red in flamboyant Italian style - taught me something of the value of 'bang' over 'buzz'. I remembered 1950s magazine reviews speaking disparagingly of the vertical twin 650cc Triumph Thunderbird as having too much of this 'buzz' for chair work; Panther 600cc and 650 cc singles, on the other hand, had 'bang'. As far as the screaming 49cc truck and the big single BSA thumper went, I preferred the science and ergonomics of the latter - also the spectacle. Heavy thuds seem to have a purpose that high screams don't, as Harley-Davidson have known for years.

The third three-wheeler that I liked fell somewhere between these two. Sometimes in Florence, far from the cultural centre in those long warrens of streets heading out to Fiesole or Prato, you would stop at traffic lights and, drawing up next to you, would be a vehicle typical of the time and disregarded by most, but studied intently by me. Its engine had a slow, regular thud which sent judders through its girder truck frame with high sides of planking. It had an attractive cab, old-fashioned in a 1950s way, generally painted grey, a cobby, steel-girder chassis with solid differential in the middle of a high grey axle, and large disc wheels - probably 21inch - with heavy, block-tread tyres. The cab was fully glazed with wind-up windows and wind-screen wiper and, inside it, usually wearing a string vest in the 35 degree centigrade temperatures of a Florentine summer, would be a laconic, dark-skinned Tuscan workman astride the front end of a Moto Guzzi horizontal-cylinder 500cc motorcycle. There he would be, gripping his handle-bars, perched on his sprung saddle with the measured chugging of the single with its large 'bacon-slicer' outside flywheel spinning by his ankle. Ahead of him were the strengthened front girder forks, flat-bladed with hefty springs, and beneath him, in this cab with no floor, the road.

As the lights changed, he clunked into gear, let out his clutch and, its note changing to a slow banging, the single piston heaved the lorry off from rest and lurched away over the cobbles and pitted tarmac, swaying from side to side with its load of bricks or marble slabs. I think that what I liked about this last of the three was the utter surrealism of the motorbike *inside* the lorry cab - as disturbing, in its way, as Magritte's fur tea-cup and saucer, but oddly satisfying too; all the interest of Moto Guzzi's iconic 'Falcone' single inside a safe, stable, private three-wheeled world. Since those days, now over thirty years ago, I recognize exactly the same characteristics interpenetrating and sustaining the creation of most motorcycle combinations and powered trikes. It's an intermingling of unlikely things into an harmonious whole.

Will you, realistically, carry a passenger very often?

In all this business of deciding which third wheel you will add to your bike, you'll notice that I haven't alluded once to the possibility that you will be carrying a passenger. This is deliberate because, most of the time, you won't. Innumerable magazine articles of the '60s extolled the passenger-carrying virtues of this sidecar or that, the ease of accessibility for mothers clutching infants, the space available for children, grannies and pets. But the fact is that nowadays you, like everyone else, will own a car - fast, silent, climate-conditioned, with seat-belts, air-bags, CD player and pollen-filters. That is where your family will want to travel, especially if any distance is to be covered. They will take initial, squealing trips in your newly-acquired sidecar or on your gleaming trike, but it

WARMTH is essential to comfort. An ex-W.D. flying-suit is ideal. If not, a sleeping bag with a hot water bottle will do the job

will be in the spirit of a theme-park ride. Soon, very soon, you will be piloting your outfit alone. Although there are a few heroes of the road who use outfits for every-day transport of relatives and children, you'll mainly only read about them in magazines, unless you join one

Note how the chair has a lifting scuttle as well as a little door. Doors are virtually unknown on today's sidecars.

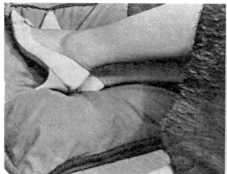

Advice from the days when a sidecar was every day transport, especially for women.

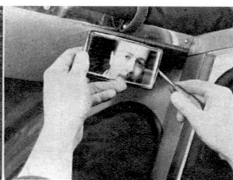

CUSHIONS are handy for passengers who wear high heels to place the feet on. It saves stiletto heels ruining the floor

MIRRORS can be fitted to most makes of sidecar and are most useful to women—for powdering noses and combing their hair

of the camping clubs for side-carrists where you will encounter some in the flesh. Most of us buy chairs or convert to trikes for our personal pleasure alone.

The modern sidecar is often a triumph of form over function; this is because function is not even a secondary consideration. It never was very high, even in the sidecar's heyday. The natural sidecar passenger was an uncomplaining, subservient woman, and, after all, her only other transport choice was to catch a bus or walk. People were a lot more used to discomfort in the early 20th century. Articles often appeared as late as in the Beatles' era extolling the virtues of packed newspaper round the sidecar passenger's feet in winter. When the wooden-framed, metal-panelled sidecar was ditched in favour of the smooth lines of fibre-glass, style became paramount, and the handling capabilities and appearance of the outfit as a whole became the focus of magazine reviews, not its sidecar's comfort. The 'how to' contributions of motorcycle journalists in mid-1960s editions of *Motorcycle, Scooter and Three-wheeler Mechanics* often featured side-car driving, but the accompanying photographs nearly always depicted the rider on his own. Wives and girlfriends had probably begun to insist on a cheap car.

Try getting into this! A modern German Tornado sports chair not really designed with a passenger's needs in mind. Form here is a long way ahead of function

As I mentioned at the beginning of this section, any motorbike can haul a chair. In the immediate post-war period Swallow Sidecars produced the 'Gadabout', a spindly trades carrier, Brockhouse offered a passenger sidecar for its very under-powered 'Indian Brave', the Garrard 'Gazelle' was sold as suitable for a bike in the 125-200cc range. Several small fibre-glass projectiles were designed for scooters, like Watsonian's 'Bambini'. Such marriages were fairly uncommon, though. Even in their day, they would have struggled to keep pace with other traffic, although it should be remembered that commercial trucks were limited to 20mph for many years and a cruising speed of 40mph was considered pretty good for a typical family saloon, like a side-valve Ford 'Popular'.

In the 1950s and '60s it was not uncommon for a chair to be hitched to a 350 single, especially if the chair was a light, sporty single-seater. The late Vic Willoughby wrote a charmingly enthusiastic review of Watsonian's new fibre-glass 'Monza' hitched to a Velocette 'Viper' for *Motorcycling*. His passenger was editor Bob Currie and they roared into Wales from Birmingham in mid-winter, and it snowed. Vic wrote that the 'Viper' got stuck into its task like a terrier after a bone, spending hour after hour in second gear, with the engine showing no sign of its labour other than an exhaust pipe glowing red-hot. In these cases of small engines the key to performance was a change of gearing - easily done in those days of near-universal chain final drive. With a final drive sprocket suitably enlarged by a few teeth, any of the popular models could transport at least a load

The author's Bullett 500 with GP sports in the mid '90s. These 'living fossils' as more than one motorcycle journalist has described them, are still available today, making an instant facsimile of a very common breed in the '50s: a 24bhp single with single-seater. Their performance is fairly 'period' too.

of two passengers. After all, the Bond mini-car was intended to seat two adults and two children and its completely enclosed body with four seats and all fitments was powered by only 122cc, later enlarged to 197cc, in the form of an air-cooled Villiers two-stroke single. A contemporary road test of the early car took two men and a child's weight of luggage from Preston, Lancashire (where the cars were built) to London. The journey took ten hours at an average 22mph. This was not thought particularly feeble, however. Right up to the death of the micro-car in the '60s, very small capacity engines were used. This was the mark of a low-wage, high fuel-cost society, of course, rather like Italy up to the late '70s. Now such vehicles are found mainly in the Third World.

The single-cylinder 500: low-powered plonk

The staple sidecar machine in Europe for a good many years was the 500cc single and it appeared in many, many forms. Each manufacturer offered its model, the frame complete with side-car lugs or bolt-holes. The engine was often a side-valve, for, although these heavy fly-wheeled motors ran hot and produced little brake horse power, they had an attractive slogging torque which suited the loping, slowish speeds expected of the outfits of the time.

If one wants such a machine today, one only has to pick up the 'phone and contact Watsonian-Squire of Moreton-in-Marsh, England. This firm, apart from producing the UK's largest range of sidecars, currently imports the old Royal Enfield 'Bullet' 350cc and 500c singles which are still manufactured in India. The latest incarnations have five speeds and electric start, with gear and brake pedals on the accepted sides, although the old opposite British arrangement can still be specified. Watsonian-Squire supply them ready fitted with suitable chairs, such as the lightweight 'Stratford' or 'GP Manx' (so called because it has no tail). I owned an Enfield 500 harnessed to a 'Jubilee' GP Sports

Classic British big singles on sports chairs. The one on the left is a Steib from the '50s, the one on the Matchless is a Watsonian GP Sports - one of the English tributes to the Zeppelin-bodied Steib, the other being Garrard's offering. Neither British sidecar offered Steib's comfortable sprung body, however.

in 1992 and the two of them went very well together. I didn't expect much in the way of performance, so I wasn't disappointed. I recall how once I pushed the motor a little too sharply in London traffic and it nipped up just outside the old Wimbledon FC ground and locked solid. After ten minutes it freed off and I never experienced the fault again. Part of the problem was the 'Albion' gear-box with its big jump between third and fourth. Third is too low, so it's happiest at 25mph, but taking it into fourth to get up to 50mpg causes pinking, especially with a passenger. I remember a review of an identical outfit in the Lake District, England, written for *Motorcycle Sport and Leisure* by Jonathan Jones. He noted the same drawback and warned about fourth gear on any but level roads: "Push things and the motor complains like a rattle-snake". The faithful bike did find its job hard and eventually wore out. An overhaul followed and it was sold as a solo for a few hundred pounds. I remember a truck driver leaning out over me on one occasion and saying: "Why can't you get a car, mate, like everyone else and stop cluttering up the road on that thing?" A bit of a cheek, I felt, coming from someone in a 40 ton juggernaut grinding through the London suburbs.

The fact is that 500s do seem slow and underpowered when pulling chairs these days. It's not so much their low top speed, although that can prove an irritant to other drivers on narrow country roads, but their lack of that vivid acceleration taken for granted by our turbo-generation of car-users. If none of this worries you, go ahead. 500 singles and smallish chairs do make a happy pairing, a bit of living history, providing you can feel un-pressured enough to pull in and let others pass. At least you know you haven't a chance of competing and, as I've suggested already, that's strangely freeing - the motoring equivalent of selling up and becoming a beach lizard far away from the rat-race.

The single-cylinder 650: classic thumpers and modern revvers

Amazingly, the big single is still alive and is produced by several of the major manufacturers, but generally of 650ccs. In my younger days, one of the commonest biking sights on British roads was the old 'Panther' 600cc or 650cc single, produced in Cleckheaton, Yorkshire, by Phelon & Moore. This bike chugged along with a giant 2/3-seater sidecar, urbanely loping round corners with hardly a change in the steady heart-beat of its piston. It was happiest at dead on 30mph, just where third gear was not screaming, and at 42mph on the level, where fourth gear let the single *just* get into a thrum, rather than a thump. 'Panthers', like the Norton 'Big 4' or other machines produced entirely with sidecar haulage in mind, had exceptionally heavy flywheels - rather like those in the softly-tuned Guzzi singles which powered the three wheeled trucks I've

Another snap of the Panther 120 attached to a Watsonian child/adult saloon. The 120 was an example of a good design over-stretched. The original Panther 100 was 600cc; stroking out to 650cc involved a reduction in flywheel diameter and as the flywheel, with a scraper, was responsible for returning oil to the sump a smaller wheel gave more sluggish re-circulation with attendant bearing and wear worries.

already touched on. Every power pulse was ironed out and the weight of the flywheels carried the whole ensemble round corners and over hump-backed bridges with ease. It's rather a pity that the vogue for big flywheels has vanished with the urge for bhp and acceleration, rather than torque.

Modern big singles, like BMW's 650 range, or the single trailies produced by the Japanese Big Four, can make quite nice sidecar machines, but they need to be treated very differently from their Panther-esque ancestors. Revs are what take the place of plonk, and their acceleration, even with a passenger in the chair, can be impressive. I write this glibly, but in fact I've only ever seen half-a-dozen modern singles on chairs, and I've tried fewer. One of these was a Suzuki 'Savage' with 'Wasp' sports chair, and it did seem to have the performance edge on the traditional Enfield 500 style of bike.

The 650 twin: The British 'standard' - more buzz than bang

Still in the 650 category, one now comes to the consideration of one of the most common classic variations of a twin-cylinder design. Purists used to say, as I have mentioned already, that a twin had too much 'buzz', ie: required too many revs, to perform satisfactorily with a sidecar, but that's only a statement of how people preferred to use the throttle. In the days of low wages when wringing every mile out of every gallon was important, the ability of a bike to perform on 'just a whiff of throttle' was a very necessary virtue. 'Grabbing a handful' to do the same task was not seen as desirable - not as far as the frugal, prudent family sidecar driver was concerned. Nowadays, it doesn't matter. It

A beautifully preserved example of 'The Gentleman's Motorcycle' - the post-war BSA Group's Sunbeam S7 500cc air-cooled twin with Watsonian Monza sidecar. Driven gently, the weakness of Erling Poppe's underslung worm final drive was not provoked into too many problems. Driven hard, it was!

should matter in an era when everyone's carbon footprint counts, but such is the spending power of the leisure *aficionado* of motorcycles in the developed countries that, however expensive gasoline becomes, it's never the prime consideration.

Older, smaller twins, like the BSA group's infamous 'Sunbeam' S7 (which, in any case, was only 500cc) were not very satisfactory sidecar machines. In the Sunbeam's case it was the under-slung worm and pinion final drive that was the Achilles heel, always a bit high-geared for haulage, incapable of being altered and having a tendency to shred metal at speed or under load. That said, BSA made a complete combo using the bike and there are a few still chugging around at moderate velocities.

The bigger BSA models, like the A10, and those classic Triumph 650s, the 'Bonneville' and its single carburettor sibling, were all pressed into sidecar work in the late 1950s and '60s and their 35 - 40bhp makes them able to hold their own today - provided they are coupled to a single-seater. A certain amount of work needs to be done to a high-revving twin in a light frame to make it work happily with a big chair, although such pairings were still not uncommon forty years ago. The oil-in-frame designs of the Umberslade

Proof that an oil-in-frame Triumph can haul a chair. This bike brought this Australian sidecar back from down-under overland when the young man next to it was a baby - and it still runs well. (Photo by kind permission of the owner)

Hall era of BSA/Triumph's last days (1970-71) were said to be unsuitable for sidecar work, but experience has proven that fears of their cracking and letting oil escape were unfounded. The Triumph oil-in-frame machines continued to be produced by the Meriden cooperative and then under licence by Harris in Devon up until the early '80s. I spoke recently at a steam and classic vehicle fair to a young man who had taken one of these late models round the world to Australia where, after the birth of his son, a big classic Aussie sidecar was fitted. Four years later, the machine was back in Britain, still being used as family transport. Should you fancy such a classic design, spares and expertise are plentiful, as are the machines themselves.

The opposed-twin 'boxers' - an enduring design

Some of the best sidecar bikes were German-made. The Germans have continued their fondness for combinations, and periodicals dedicated to this specialised area of the market still exist. The famous Zundapp and BMW 750cc outfits which carried three German soldiers and their armaments across North African desert and Russian plain were among the most specialised adaptations of the sidecar idea. With forward and reverse gears, driven sidecar wheel and immensely rigid construction they illustrated what could be done with a softly-tuned motor (producing only 25bhp) with the right transmission and fork/frame design. I'm going to touch on this business of how a combination should best be steered later. There's a lot of heat and opinion about this in specialist circles which centres on the belief that telescopic forks are not suited to three-wheel work. I've never agreed with this view, and I believe that quite a few people go to the expense of fitting leading-link forks unnecessarily. However, to get back to the WWII battle-wagon

Left an early '70s Russian Ural M66 650 boxer - the bike that got the author into sidecars. Right…and it's still available today - in this case with shaft driven right hand sidecar, technically illegal on UK roads. Unpowered LH-fitting chairs are also available with the greatly improved modern Ural.

The real thing: a 1942 Zundapp military outfit with shaft-drive from rear wheel to chair clearly visible.

outfits, it's worth mentioning that they are extremely rare and almost never come up for sale, and are very costly when they do. But, should your fancy turn in this direction, there is an alternative.

The nearest modern-day equivalent is the range of 650/750cc boxer twins produced in Russia by Ural (Ypar) and in China by Chang-Jiang, the former of which is a better bet in terms of build-quality and spares. The current importers of the UralMoto franchise, like F2 Motorcycles of Banbury in Britain (and for Chang Jiang BEMW), sell these machines complete with sidecar - usually modelled on the WWII Steib metal military model. Reliability is greatly improved on the machines of the old USSR which were originally imported in the early 1970s. I bought one of these early M66 bikes in 1972 from Fred Wells of London and had it fitted with a Watsonian 'Monza' chair by Munday's of Brixton. This proved too light for it and was exchanged for a giant Busmar 'Astral'. This chair, nick-named 'the tomb' by a friend, lived up to its name by pulling off its bolts on a steep hill in Wimbledon, London with him inside it, and tumbling away down the slope filled with his shrieks of terror. The M66 was then fitted to a stupendously heavy Ural chair, in matching bright blue, and on the 'wrong' side. In this guise I took it down through Italy on a trip which featured over thirty breakdowns (mainly caused, though I didn't know it at the time, by the lack of a

proper heat-stopping gasket between carburettor and cylinder which caused premature evaporation of fuel in the hot Italian summer). This sidecar's body was abandoned in Tuscany in my mother's garage and the Ural came back to the UK attached only to its frame, upon which the girl to whom I was engaged had to stand to keep it down on the Alpine hairpins. A case of true love. The bike was eventually stolen while in my brother's custody, but I have a perverse, nostalgic hankering for it still. Should you buy a new Ural combo today, I can guarantee you will grow fond of it, as I did.

The author bringing his Ural back over the Alps from Italy with chassis only in 1973. Mechanical troubles had forced abandonment of the heavy sidecar body.

Modern BMW 1200cc cruiser fitted (not without difficulty owing to the absence of a traditional frame) to a colour matched Watsonian-Squire GP. This sort of project illustrates the ingenuity of sidecar manufacturers. You will find they don't know the meaning of the word 'can't' when it comes to fitment.

Modern 1150 and 1200 'boxers': a challenge to pair with a chair

Civilian boxers (horizontally-opposed twins) were rather the province of the BMW marque and their copies. BMW continue to make them in large capacity form. Classic bike collectors consider the post-war period as the definitive one for these machines, and a bike from this period (up to about 1963) complete with Earles leading-link forks and matching Steib chair is still a treat for the eyes. Modern 1200cc and 1150cc frameless BMW boxers *can* be fitted with sidecars, but, as I found out when speaking to the owner of one such last year, it is a complex business, requiring - in his case - quite a lot of expense and ingenuity from Watsonian-Squire. But it was done, it's rigid and handsome, goes well, and he loves it. Unit Sidecars make a special trials-like tall chair for the latest BMW 'enduro' twins and have overcome, by clever design, all the problems which arise on a virtually frameless machine.

The V-twin: the ideal sidecar configuration?

As this implies, it is the capacities above 750cc which interest most sidecar purchasers these days. Ever since the Brough 'Superior' and chair proclaimed itself in the Rolls Royce category in the mid 1930s, many have regarded the large-capacity V-twin as the ideal sidecar machine. Luckily there are now a large number of these types of bikes to choose from. This is partly due to the undying popularity of Harley-Davidsons and that

Sidecars have come a long way since this wickerwork Clyno combo was made before WWI. Its construction is why, of course, sidecars are called 'chairs'. The long wheel-base V-twin is still thought by many to be the ideal form for a sidecar tug.

most sincere form of flattery - a desire to emulate - on the part of most of the world's other big players. Harleys make very good sidecar machines, their belt-drive notwithstanding. These belts are immensely strong, are toothed and don't stretch, so you need have no fears that yours will break under the heavier loads imposed by chair work. Any of the Harley range can be easily attached to a sidecar, although the V-Rod needs more welding because its configuration of heavy tubing makes clamping less easy. This model is the only one in the Harley line-up which has much greater bhp than torque, thanks to the Porsche-designed motor, so is theoretically less well adapted to haulage than the standard 1450cc Evolution motor found in the Dyna-glide, Fat Boy, Electra-Glide, Road King and other 'Springer' and 'Softail' models. These have conventional tubed frames and that long wheel-base and lazy engine, with more torque than bhp, which suits haulage. The 1200 Sportster also works well with a single-seat chair. All Harley-esque designs which have silencers on the right-hand side of the bike particularly

Vincent HRD 998cc V-twin with Steib chair. A combo like this was top of the range in 1951.

Today's imposing equivalent to the Vincent
opposite, the Harley Road King V-twin on a
Unit Hedingham XL

suit pairing with a sidecar in countries which drive on the left. In their native North America the pipes lie between chair and bike, of course, making for a loud journey for any passenger.

I have yet to see a 'Victory' with a sidecar on either side of the pond, but I should imagine that making a combo with one would be similar to doing so with a Harley. They have similar configurations and engine characteristics, although the Victory is quite high-geared. Its hefty displacement and massive torque should make easy work of pairing up, I would imagine.

In the 1950s in Britain, the Vincent 998cc V-twin was considered the best possible side-carrist's ideal and testers of the period revelled in its power and luxury. A reviewer of a Vincent 'Rapide' and Blacknell 'Sherwood' child-adult pointed out, in *Motorcycling* May 1951, that the outfit 'provides a performance, coupled with passenger comfort, which would cost [very much more] if the vehicle had a wheel at each corner instead of two in-line and one at the side'. Even though the front passenger can 'get in or out without disarranging her hat', the rear seat can seat two children in comfort and the sidecar is 'snug in winter', (although 'with only a small hood-flap to provide ventilation, it might become too warm if heavy rain necessitated complete battening-down in midsummer') it is unlikely that modern travellers would prefer it to a car!

The natural successors of this fabled and unobtainable machine (although Vincent fans might be loath to agree!) now lie in the V-twin ranges of the big Japanese manufacturers and many of these bikes assemble into marvellous outfits. There's a big size range available too, from 800cc to 2000cc. They are all cruiser-like in style with a conventional cradle frame and long wheel-base. Most have outputs in the 60bhp - 90bhp

The distinctive Brough 4, designed specifically for sidecar haulage with its twin rear wheels and water cooled Austin 7 four-cylinder engine. It was claimed that it could be ridden solo. Brough's JAP and Matchless engined V-twins on Brough's own fuel-in-frame sidecar were very highly regarded in the 1930s.

range - higher than a well-fettled Brough or Vincent from the past - and they all have excellent torque figures, some higher than 140lb-ft. While some use belt-drive in imitation of Harley-Davidson, the majority favour shafts and these are also particularly apt for conversion to trikes. The shaft output is taken, via a specially made-up prop-shaft, to the rear axle.

The machine I've often seen bolted to a chair is Yamaha's XVS1100 DragStar - a model offered, as I've mentioned already - by Watsonian-Squire ready equipped with a GP sports 1½ seater. The virtues of this bike are well-known across the world, especially in continental Europe where it, and its smaller 650cc brother, were the best-selling cruisers in the late '90s. The 1100cc version has more flexible 'bang', I think (I've had outfits based on both models), is capable of turning over very slowly, as when taking sharp left-handers in London traffic in second gear, is easy to work on (apart from a maddening need to remove the exhaust when changing the oil filter - a necessity which must be extra-infuriating when your chair is on the right-hand side of the bike), is shaft-driven and has a heavy old-fashioned frame suitable for taking clamps or welded lugs.

Yamaha's 'Road Star', once sold in the UK as the 'Wild Star', was a 1600cc push-rod design of similar bhp to the 1100cc 'DragStar', but with twice the torque. Also simple and air-cooled, with belt-drive instead of shaft, it too makes a fine sidecar bike. In 2006 it was uprated to 1700cc. Its successors in Yamaha's range use versions of the same massive air-cooled V-twin, the 1854cc art-deco 'Stratoliner' ('Midnight Star' in the UK) looking tempting, although its aluminium frame needs investigation before a chair is attached. The liquid-cooled 1300's frame is steel.

The author's Drag Star XVS 1100A Classic fitted to a Unit Hedingham Sprite. This small retro-styled chair goes well with the flowing tin-ware of this particular cruiser model.

Suzuki have always had a great chair bike in the big 'Intruder' range. The 1400cc custom machine has also been a favourite with trike builders. Suzuki, too, have extended the basic displacements of their big V-twins to create the top-of-the-range 'Boulevard' models. In C90 form, this bike is a delightful, gentle wafter; the M109 has the liquid-cooled motor upped to 1783cc. The Honda VTX 1800, like the Suzuki, is also water-cooled. Like its smaller 1300cc sibling, it's great on a chair with car-like tractability, though it's high-geared. Kawasaki's Vulcan 903cc and 2053cc bikes have immense potential for three-wheeled use. The original 1500cc water-cooled Kawasaki Classic cruiser was one of the most popular choices for sidecar haulage in the '90s.

All these Japanese bikes make fantastic second-hand bargains, are plentiful, easily serviced throughout the world, ultra-reliable and beautifully finished. As a general rule-of-thumb, I've found that Yamaha's machines are the most finely-detailed, with the best bodywork finish and Honda's the most mechanically competent and refined. You'll notice that I've homed in on the naked, retro, cruiser-styled end of the respective manufacturers' ranges. Plenty of people fit sidecars to the sportier bikes in each of these makers' line-ups. I've never tried a chair on an out-and-out sports machine, but Charnwood Classic Restorations and Merlin Sidecars in Britain supply sports/sidecar combos of amazing power. Nick Payne wrote an amusing review of one in *Motorcycle Sport and Leisure* when, in 1999, Charnwood were first creating Honda Super Blackbird and Suzuki Hayabusa outfits. 'The aggressive-looking plot might have originated on a different planet,' he wrote. 'It surges forward in any gear; it'll even spin the rear wheel at 90mph in third. In the dry too. Give it its head and it becomes manic.' It isn't quite my idea of stress-free sidecarring, but it just shows that everything's possible.

The peculiar aptness of the modern V-twin for sidecar work

One characteristic I've noticed about many of the big Japanese cruisers is that they don't have any problems running straight without wobbles. It is a characteristic of placing a chair alongside a machine that, because of the geometry of the steering front wheel and its trail, the handle-bars can oscillate at low speeds or when decelerating. This 'wheel-wobble' was always eradicated in the past by screwing down a simple friction damper which nipped-up the steering-head bearing. Modern bikes don't have such dampers, so if your sidecar outfit wobbles you need to buy a hydraulic cylinder damper and fit it with clamps between one of your fork legs and the sidecar chassis. These completely cure the problem, but are a pain in the neck in other respects. They inhibit the full lock (especially away the chair) which is such a nice part of sidecar-driving. In all countries this turn away from the sidecar is precisely where you need to do a nifty U-turn to get out of a traffic jam. It's a lot less fun trying to do this with restricted lock and no reverse gear, paddling with both feet to get the outfit back out of the camber like a frantic swan. Also a fixed damper is another thing to have to remove and then re-adjust if you like to re-convert your bike quickly to solo use. The point I realise that I'm laboriously making is that almost none of these big Japanese V-twin cruisers needs a damper. I've been wobbled until my fillings rattled on Royal Enfields and BSAs, for example, but not on outfits made with Kawasaki Classic 1500s, Suzuki Intruders or Yamaha Stars. I can't think why, especially as their trail is not particularly favourable for chair work. There is more about all this later in the section about modifications (see pages 117-118).

The high performance sports-replica: an exhilarating handful, on track or street

There are other machines in the big category (up to 2000cc) which make interesting side-car tugs, but, as I have mentioned when referring to the violently fast outfits made by Merlin and others, these are generally not twins and have engine characteristics very different from those of the V-twin Harley/Brough/Vincent ancestry. If you own a fast sports bike, it will probably be an in-line four. It will also be light and capable of high revs. Such machines, with their racing posture and the considerable adaptation of gearing, steering and braking, and the particular problems associated with attaching sidecar mounts

The Suzuki Bandit 1200 in-line four is quite often seen on capacious sidecars, as with this EML-inspired Squire. This bike has been fitted with leading link forks. Note the solid car wheel conversion at the rear. This lowers gearing and gives strength.

through all-enclosing plastic bodywork to virtually frameless inner construction, are for the very single-minded and dedicated sports sidecarrist who will, almost certainly, whizz along at inter-stellar speeds on his magnificent aberration alone.

The 'car on two wheels'

Then there is the *Ubertourer*, the Honda GoldWing, an evergreen which has gone through four- and six-cylinder development, growing larger and larger all the time. It, and its naked cruiser cousin (which ceased production in 2006) the F6C or Valkyrie, are often attached to sidecars and they do make obvious partners for one. They are a handful to keep upright unsupported. This is why so many firms offer them in triked versions too. I personally find the bike overwhelms the chair in most incarnations, although a Watsonian Cambridge manages to hold its own. What these giants need is the re-manufacture of those enormous Canterbury Carmobile three-seaters from the early '60s which, in their day, hopelessly overwhelmed their little BSA A10 or Triumph 650 partners. This is utterly unlikely to happen, of course, so I would recommend that the two or three year-old F6C you are thinking of making into a stable three-wheeler be turned into a handsome trike.

The option for the monstrous

Beyond the 1100 - 2000cc range of bikes lie the fascinating mountain peaks of *really* big motorcycles. Now obviously a machine in the 11-1200cc range, weighing 280kg, with a wheelbase of 1600mm, 62bhp and torque of 70ft-lb, is more than adequate for sensible and 'real-world' sidecar driving. Such a bike - like a Harley Dynaglide or Yamaha DragStar- is going to be easy to fix, reliable, eye-catching, fast enough fully loaded and, in traffic, flexible enough to be manoeuvrable. It is not going to need huge adaptation to steering, frame or forks, and not much to its suspension (more about suspension tweaks later). But if such a machine doesn't appeal to you and you must have something near the outside edge, then the Triumph Rocket III must be a candidate. With 2.3 litres and vast amounts of bhp and torque, this three-cylinder, in-line, shaft-driven behemoth, with power characteristics closer to the bigger type of executive saloon, but only weighing 320kg, comes close to the largest motorcycle that can be ridden in all conditions, comfortably. In 2006, this, the largest production bike in the world, became an instant icon. Partnering it with a decent-sized chair is a marriage made in heaven - so thought

All variants of Kawasaki's large capacity cruisers make light work of having a chair fitted. Here the 1500cc Drifter is mated to the ubiquitous Watsonian-Squire Jubilee. Kawasaki's original 1500cc V-twin Classic cruiser, right up to the new 2000cc Mean Streak have the strong frames and capable water-cooled motors needed for long-distance three-wheeled touring.

The Triumph Rocket III is currently the largest volume production motorcycle at 2300cc. Unit sidecars have fitted it to an enlarged version of their Hedingham XL chair, complete with their leading-link forks. This three cylinder machine, with its car like qualities of torque and power, will no doubt become increasingly popular with chair and trike fanciers. (With kind permission of Outlook *magazine)*

Unit sidecars of Sible Hedingham, England, and their prototype Hedingham XL adapted for the Rocket III, matches it extremely well. I'd also like to see what the Rocket looks like connected to the 1½ seat version of Watsonian's GP Sports Jubilee. With water-cooling, this large combo should not get fazed if caught in the odd traffic jam on a hot day (not that this upsets air-cooled bikes either these days, probably because of their finning - so much more generous than that of '60s bikes) and, with a track larger than a Bentley, it *will* get caught. Yet what an eye-opening outfit it is! One would need deep pockets for this, of course: the bike is twice the price of the cheapest cars and the fitment and purchase of the chair might easily add a further 40% to the overall cost. What a way to spend a bit of that retirement lump sum! Remember, however, that these big Triumphs lose 22% of their value in a year, much more after three years, so purchase of a good second-hand bike and new colour-matched chair would probably be the sensible way forward.

Now comes the far, far edge of utter insanity in the world of motorcycle combinations. While the Rocket III is currently the world's largest production bike, as I have mentioned already, it probably will not remain so for long. There is always kudos in bagging that particular title. But no one is likely to catch up with a low-volume producer whose bike is so extreme that to own one would be a very pronounced statement of non-conformity indeed. I am referring, of course, to the Boss Hoss from Tennessee, USA, a machine

The Far Side. A V8 Chevy-powered 5.8 litre Boss Hoss. No photo prepares you for the impact of one of these in the metal. Often seen in triked form - and Boss Hoss themselves offer it in various formats - it is available with a sidecar from Armec America. Three wheels are really needed to keep it upright.

originally of 5700cc in V8 formation, producing 345bhp and having a dry weight of 500kg. It rides on a 12 inch wide car rear tyre and can roar up to 170mph on its one gear. Its designer, Monty Warne, created a cruiser-style fuel tank three feet across by using two Harley tanks welded together. This was back in the early '90s. Now, the Boss Hoss is available in new 6 litre and small bore(!) sizes and, if one goes to the Daytona *Bikefest*, can be seen triked and with sidecars. It's only sense to have such a beast supported by a third wheel. What might happen if you were trapped beneath that hot Chevy V8 hardly bears thinking about. 2008 emission laws saw the end of the ancient iron 502 cu.in. The 'small' alloy 364 cu.in Corvette motor still gives 425bhp *and* loses 280 lbs in weight.

Naturally, this machine from the far edges of the possible, has been partnered with a chair. The Swiss firm of Armec has created a strengthened version of its Tremola sidecar for the purpose - available from Armec of America. It makes a jaw-dropping sight, but perfectly controllable, thanks to the amazingly docile flexibility of the smooth, massive V8. If money were absolutely no object, if one could get the thing serviced easily wherever one lived and if one could persuade one of the UK sidecar firms to match it with a chair for use on the left (for Armec only cater for the right-hand drive countries), and if one could swallow the counter-belief that global warning is just a myth, then one might *just* have to have one - if only to be one of the few on the planet to do so.

What a choice – but if only there were a diesel too....

So, there we are. From a 125cc scooter up to a six litre juggernaut, there's a bike/chair combination somewhere for you. To those who think that fitting a sidecar to a motorcycle manages to create the worst of both worlds of car and bike, I would posit the opposite argument. What is created is the *best* of both. You have a lot of the small, open sports car's stability, safety, carrying capacity and visibility - and with a large dose of entertaining eccentricity thrown in; you have a bike's open-air sense of freedom and individuality, the age-old sensation of riding your own horse and - unless you plump for a Boss Hoss - some of a bike's narrow track and nippy manoeuvrability. It is, as ever, horses for courses, and the future may throw up fascinating alternatives, like a developed version of the big Neander diesel cruiser, currently a prototype.

The time must surely come when a diesel-engined motorcycle becomes something more than an industrial single of 8bhp bolted into an Enfield chassis, which is what Ernie Dorsett and then the 'Robin Enfield' gave us. Such machines, while jolly in a time-capsule, B-road sort of way, could never be adapted to sidecar use. They can barely haul themselves around. Their 200 mpg consumption is unlikely to be matched by a turbo diesel of more than 1500cc, which is the sort of future the Neander is looking at, but averages in the 70-80mpg area have got to be better than the 35-40 which current large-capacity petrol bikes give us. I like automatic cars and I'd welcome an auto diesel motorcycle with enough performance to take a chair or be triked, if desired. I'm sure I would not be alone.

Not a diesel, just plain bizarre - the one-off Red Bull Royal Enfield and adapted GP Manx. The low, rakish screen and twin light mudguard greatly improve the lines of the GP Manx sidecar. (Photo: Watsonian-Squire)

Cap'n Sensible's choice

If forced to make a recommendation now for someone else in the middle of that spectrum from scooter to Boss Hoss, I would plump for what I myself (in spite of veering in either direction on occasions) have been happy with for the last ten years: a 900cc - 1200cc softly-tuned V-twin hitched to a light, single-seat sports chair. The great thing is to be realistic about all those parameters of use. A really vast, rare, expensive outfit is never the best choice for popping to shops or using in town or round country roads, and fuel consumption has some bearing on choice; so have servicing availability and insurance costs. Unless you are setting off for a long tour of Europe, or a transcontinental US voyage, it makes sense to think medium. My current combo, at the time of writing, consists of a Yamaha DragStar XVS1100 with a Unit Hedingham Sprite chair, bought in 2006, and I'm pretty happy with it for the humdrum tasks that I use it for: town, suburban and A-road driving for both work and occasional fun spins all the year round. When I replace it, I'll probably go for something similar, keeping the sane side of 1600cc with a narrow-tracked single-seat sports chair.

The Moto Guzzi California makes an excellent, strong sidecar machine. The transverse V-twin is in a gentle state of tune with tons of torque. Its modern variant is considered less tractor like, but the original - only just discontinued - has chunky charm. The chair is a colour matched Hedingham XL.

WHAT ABOUT A TRIKE?

Going for a third wheel can, naturally, involve making a trike of your motorcycle. This option is remarkably popular in America and shows signs of taking off (in a modest fashion) in the UK as well. I was exchanging e-mails with a journalist friend on *The Los Angeles Times* recently about a planned visit of his to Britain. He asked if he could bring me anything from stateside and I, having heard that a new magazine was being launched called *Trike*, asked him to bring me a copy. After failing to find anyone who had even heard of it, my friend then found out that the reason it wasn't available in Los Angeles was that it was British! I thought that was most interesting and encouraging.

The problem with trikes....

A few years ago the idea of a trike in the UK had distinctly un-inclusive connotations: it seemed to bring to mind one of those predominantly black and rusty concoctions of steel girders with Reliant or Cortina engines, overwhelmed-looking Suzuki front forks and a bizarre edifice of planks, boxes, wrought iron and swastikas at the rear. The whole thing was often topped off by stickers like: 'F*ck with this F*cker's ride an' you get F*cked' or 'Gay Satanist Bikers' Action Group'. This Brit version of the severely deranged Vietnam vet' also drove bare-headed with studded leather waistcoat, in tiny black shades

This sort of 'trike' has powerful qualities which may not engage everyone interested in three wheels. It is a Ford Cortina powered 5-wheeler of imposing size, but Forth Bridge-like industrial construction. Those stub exhausts are loud. To have a machine like this is to make a certain statement.

By contrast with the trike on the previous page, this US-styled trike is a bike-based conversion of a Honda GoldWing. With its neat, factory finished coachwork, it is much more likely to be the face of future trike trends in Europe and the UK. It's not, however, the sort of adaptation that is easily undertaken at home, although kits do exist.

and with tattoos bulging and grey locks streaming in the wind. It was not an image to be locked into very easily - especially if you wanted to ride your trike in cords, pink shirt and Davida helmet. Nik Samson, editor of the above-mentioned *Trike* magazine, often compares the self-assembled 'rat' trike to a blend of Victorian bedstead and 1930s central heating system. Apart from the aptness of his simile, I'm reassured by this note of disapproval in the UK's only trike mag. If every trike were indeed a hideous lash-up of scaffolding poles, 1970's Jap bike bits from the breaker's yard, and bellowing, un-silenced Mark I Cortina motor, the trike movement would forever remain in the corner with maypole dancers - but less popular. Unfortunately, the fatal combination of terminal non-conformity and lack of ready money has produced a fair number of these machines; indeed for most observers they *are* what is meant by a trike nowadays. I live in hope that change is on the way.

The National Association of Bikers with a Disability (NABD), founded over twenty years ago in Manchester, England, has made trike construction rather more mainstream - if with other correlatives about use. For example, no one would feel quite at ease

piloting one of the new Martin-Conquest trikes (illustrated on p52) if not in a wheel-
chair, for which it is designed, however attractive the vehicle itself might be in its own
right. The word is that this firm may manufacture a non wheel-chair version of its stunning
BMW-based design. If it does so, it may be one of the few UK-sourced computer-designed,
all-encompassing bodywork bike-based trikes available. The majority of professionally
manufactured British trikes are minimalist trans-axle conversions - often attractive in an
uncomplicated way, but not giving the impression of a vehicle designed as a unitary
whole. The most visually-impressive trikes are often one-off custom jobs, made for show
purposes with little regard for manufacturing hours or cost.

Still, creeping between these three rather different reasons for triking: the gothic
social-exclusion statement, the provision for disablement and the artistic expression in
metal, there has come a slow but steady trickle of Stateside-style leisure trikes into
Europe. These machines, usually based on top-of-the-range cruisers or tourers, are as
smart and neatly engineered as their owners' high-quality car.

That '30s central-heating system of twenty years ago was home-made, a thing of
shreds and patches, often finding it difficult to get through Britain's stringent Ministry of
Transport (MoT) Test, or Single Vehicle Approval. Donor vehicles of choice were the
original Volkswagen air-cooled Beetle, Reliant Regal or Robin microcar, but *aficionados*
mounted every type of car engine into girder frames, creating some monstrous and eye-
catching devices the appeal of which was to the grotesque rather than the aesthetic. It
really is pretty difficult to make a lovely trike in the private backyard or shed. The shape
of the machine itself, its arrangement of seats, the relationship between massive rear
differential, axle and wheels and spindly fork and front end, and the inter-linkage of
motor, gearbox, pedals, tank, electrics and transmission all present severe difficulties to
the home constructor. If he or she is content to ride around on an eccentric, dodgy-

*The simplest way of making
a trike. Keep the bike stock
(in this case a Honda F6C
flat six-cylinder cruiser) and
replace the rear wheel with
an axle. It can be reversed
fairly easily, if necessary for
re-sale.*

A super neat Harley-Davidson conversion with belt drive transmission.

looking bodge-up then the unlikeliness of the components won't necessarily prevent the thing moving along - quite rapidly in all probability. But it's getting it to *look* right as well that is the problem.

One design of lasting attraction is the Morgan style of three-wheeler with exposed motorcycle engine at the front driving one wheel at the rear. Although at their height before WWII, with V-twin motors made by JAP (J A Prestwich) and Matchless among others, replicas of these snug two-seaters keep popping up. JZR and Lomax advertised quite widely in the mid-'90s, the latter favouring the 2CV engine from Citroen's iconic

A BMW 1150 boxer given a little more bodywork than some, and a top box for storage. The trouble with trikes generally is that, unlike sidecar outfits, there is little space to put things.

basic car. Honda, Harley and Moto Guzzi mechanics have been harnessed to power these look-alikes. One of the reasons that these trikes are liked is that the bodywork is smooth, classic and, even when provided in kit form, looks professional. However, this sort of vehicle has a steering-wheel and is not, to my mind, a *real* tricycle.

What a 'proper' trike should be like

I believe implicitly that no trike looks as it should unless it is based upon a true motorcycle rather than a car's rear-end, middle or bodywork. This is because you need the correct motorcyclist's stance aboard your trike if you are going to be able to see and steer with the ease you expect on your bike. Also, if the thing is going to have any mobility at all, it needs to possess the short wheelbase of a bike. This is especially important for U-turns and parking. It's true that a car-engined trike gives you a built-in reverse gear *gratis*, as it were, but a lighter bike-derivation can be easily pushed or paddled into place, as one has to with a sidecar outfit. In any case reverse mechanisms acting on the transmission can now be specified from trike builders.

That yawning space between front wheel and rear power unit on a trike with a Volkswagen engine/transmission set-up just does not look right. There needs to be an engine under the fuel tank! An attractively-proportioned tricycle needs to be as cobby as a three-legged stool, with none of that elongated spideriness of empty frames or teetering forks which are so often the hall-marks of car-based designs.

There are plenty of firms which offer to trike your machine very simply indeed. Where the bike's rear wheel once went would soon become the home of a standard re-conditioned Ford transaxle held in suspension units mounted on out-riggers from the bike's rear frame. Drive is often taken by prop-shaft from the existing engine's gearbox output to the differential. Mudguards or fenders with lights and indicators complete the conversion, and the motorcycle, with its rider's and pillion's saddle in its usual place, can be used as normal.

Sometimes this sort of conversion looks a little temporary; it's hard to fill that curved space under the bike's rear tin-ware where the rear wheel once was and where the smaller 'blob' of the differential sits. The ensemble very much depends on the original design of the bike for its effectiveness. I've written that it looks temporary, but it isn't. There is a lot of work ahead of anyone who wishes to return most adapted machines to solo form, mainly because the outrigger attachments to hold the axle and suspension need to be welded on to parts of the bike's frame. One UK customs outfit, TAB Customs

The progenitor of all those bike conversions US Style: a Harley-Davidson Servicar, favoured by police forces in America, especially in San Francisco, as witness this SFPD trike with Electra-Glide front.

of Doncaster, which specialises in 'DragStar' conversions, simply removes the cruiser's rear end and replaces it with a bolt-on hard-tail style frame and transaxle, but that's a little unusual.

The custom and trike scene in the UK is still closely knit, so it's no surprise that a fair number of the trike workshops are also custom bike ones too. Several firms offer to build anything you wish from your stock bike - and that includes a third wheel. In all, 24 builders are spread across the UK at the time of writing and many of these are NABD accredited. A few will make one-off combos as well as tricycles. None is particularly well-known outside the custom bike/trike scene, but the quality of the best is well up to OEM standards.

What do you require from a trike?

The choice of trike layout really decides which firm you opt for. Some make or import car-derived trikes, such as the Boom or Recaro trikes which are of the VW-engineered type which I have already touched on; others use a second-hand or new bike as their basis for adaptation. It is these which, I think, make the most useful and motorcycle-like vehicles. Prices are roughly similar to the cost of a small sports sidecar - starting at around £5,000 at current prices. For that, your standard bike will be given a car rear axle and differential (often of Ford manufacture) with brakes and hubs to suit, mudguards, wheels and tyres of your choice and all the associated suspension, framework, welding and choice of drive - usually, as I have suggested, a prop-shaft. Some firms are happy to provide belt or chain drive, but the general consensus is that the extra weight of the axle and wheels can give a chain or belt a hard time. Nothing's worse than constantly having to adjust chain tension, and it's by no means easy to incorporate this facility into a tricycle. Modern belts, of the Kevlar, Harley-type are unlikely to fail early on in life, but when they do, it's a disassembly job to replace them.

When specifying work to be done it is useful to have in mind what the trike will be used for. To dart around town, you don't need trunk space or luggage racks. To undertake long tours you will, and extra fuel capacity as well. To carry just yourself and an occasional passenger, the host bike's dual-seat can be left as it is, but at extra cost a bench seat over the axle is commonly fitted. This will require seat-belt attachments by law in Britain. An important tip is to ensure it is angled back a little, as in a car, so that sharp braking doesn't pitch the passenger forward.

Although hyper-wide wheels are favoured by the exhibitionist custom triker, shod with monstrous tyres to match, these are actually not helpful to the feel and manoeuvrability of the vehicle and can scuff and scrabble annoyingly on corners.

A Harley Sportster bike conversion. The cobby short-wheelbase triangle of such adaptations is very attractive and makes for a nippy, compact machine, easy to park, manoeuvre - and push, if necessary.

EML's Martinique conversion of the ubiquitous Honda GoldWing (supplied by Colin Appleyard Motorcycles Ltd) is a perfect illustration of the best type of professional bike conversion. Beautifully detailed, with workmanship and design of the highest order, ExtensoDive suspension, bold, swooping bodywork and the easy power of the Honda engine, this is streets away from the home-bodged 'rat-trike' which used to be all one saw on UK roads a decade or so ago. (Photo courtesy Colin Appleyard Ltd)

This conversion of the Yamaha 1600cc Wild Star makes an interesting stab at filling those gaps each side of the stock rear mudguard with matched saddle bags. Note the strong, multi-spoked wheels.

It's better, I believe, to specify ordinary car-width rear tyres. They produce less power-sapping friction and generate less tiring noise at speed too. Have a look at a Harley Servicar, an American trike in production for more than 40 years; it has tyres of optimum width. The front wheel is best made of cast metal rather than spokes. Short, stubby spokes on a 15 inch wheel - the sort of thing which comes standard on a Moto Guzzi EV1100 California, can cope with the side-forces of cornering quite well, but a skinny 21 inch Harley-Davidson Night Train wheel may have the long spokes snapping under spirited cornering with a load on board. The same can apply to sidecar work, although, if you think about it, an outfit responds differently in corners in that on turns into the chair, the chair can begin to lift, taking side-load off the wheel, and in the other direction the chair suspension sinks and the bike's rear suspension rises, also absorbing load. On a trike the out-rigger wheels do not have this tendency to rise, the shape of the plot being a triangle, and the axle heavy. The front wheel is more stressed.

The great advantage of having your trike doctored at its rear end only is that you can leave the front end alone. The steering geometry and rake of the stock machine is perfectly capable of making a sweet-steering, nimble trike and (as when considering keeping the stock forks for sidecar work) the hefty nature of today's offerings on pretty well all standard bikes makes replacement unnecessary. Incidentally, a leading-link fork, often regarded as an improvement with a sidecar (with reason when replacing the spindly forks of a 'classic' machine) is less so in trike format - although many claim that its fitment can lighten up the steering by quite a helpful amount. So often the perceived heaviness of steering is actually affected more by handle-bar width than anything else, so all trikes should have wide bars as a matter of course. If you are lucky with your conversion, you won't need a steering-damper either.

Several of the UK trike makers will, as I have mentioned, fit a reverse gear at extra cost. Sometimes this is an electric one, sometimes it will be integral with the limited-slip differential. Although it's fun to be able to go backwards - especially when people are looking - if your trike is light enough you probably won't need to. It's surprising how adept one becomes with a trike or sidecar outfit at using cambers and slopes to fit into parking spaces.

The latest idea - the two-wheels-at-the-front scoot. Is this the future?

There is a way into three wheels which is neither through the addition of a sidecar, nor conversion to a trike. The motoring press has been reporting lately (2007) on the slow, but fascinating, growth of a new breed of three-wheelers which have their single wheel at the rear. Piaggio, the scooter manufacturers of Pontedera, Italy, started the ball rolling with its MP3 250cc scooter with linked, twin front wheels. It has been phenomenally successful in its home country, but is not suitable, thanks to its small motor, for main road work. Gilera (owned by Piaggio) has brought out the 500cc Fuoco 500ie, a better proposition using the same technology. Although the 40bhp engine has to lug along 250 kilos it can get up to decent speeds. It has an automatic box, like most big scooters, and isn't much wider than a Yamaha T-Max. Unlike a sidecar outfit or conventional trike, the scooter leans like a solo on bends, a brilliant linked system letting the twin front wheels lean with the bike, while each remains on the road. Tests have reported that the sensation of piloting these scooters on wet or oily surfaces is quite eerie for a motorcyclist because the machine remains so stable and just won't skid or slip. The 500 is currently (in 2008) £5,500, the 250 £4,300, and you could get a lot of bigger bikes for the money, but the idea is sensational and may well catch on, especially as the Piaggio MP3 LT, available in 2009, has a front track of 465mm and although equipped with 250cc or 400cc engines, can be ridden by holders of a normal car licence.

Why do most trikes have their single wheel at the front?

After all, although having the single wheel at the front and the twin wheels at the back seems to be the current orthodoxy, it was not always so. The earliest three-wheeled forecars, which placed their passenger on a seat in front of the driver, used a driven rear wheel with steerable front ones. Many trades carrier machines, like the popular DOT, aped the pedal-powered carrier and put their load over twin front wheels. Morgan, in

The Piaggio MP3 three-wheeled leaning scooter. This design has recently caught on in Europe and is one of the most fascinating ways in which much-needed stability is being engineered into a motorcycle.

the UK, made outstanding sporting two-seat tricycles in the 1920s and '30s, using V-twin JAP (J A Prestwich) or Matchless motorcycle engines. They proved, by convincing performances on the track, that such a layout had inherently greater stability at speed than its alternative.

It was the buying of Raleigh's Karryall design - a bike-fronted van - by T. Williams which implanted the single front wheel design in British minds. From these beginnings came the famous Reliant Company, for most Brits *the* quintessential three-wheeler. The story goes that those Raleigh machines had an 'R' cast into the crank cases, so another word beginning with this letter had to be found for the fledgling firm. The van, naturally, was used for loads, and the twin wheels were more obviously sited at the rear. Yet so great was the influence of this configuration of Reliant's, that its peers (and imitators), like BSA, James, Bond, Gordon and AC, followed the same route. It only needed Harley-Davidson to do the same in the USA with the police 'Servicar' for the future fate of world triking to be determined.

Morgan-style car-like trikes have come and gone on the UK market - such as Lomax and TriKing, variously making use of Citroen 2CV and Moto Guzzi V-twin motors, but no manufacturer has yet tried to make a *bike*-conversion with twin-steer at the front. Surely it would be a lot cheaper and easier for our custom builders and their customers, when undertaking a bike-conversion exercise, to leave the rear end alone and simply replace the forks with a bar and mud-guarded, braked wheels on stub-axles for front steering, wouldn't it?

Watch out for the 'Spyder'

Small trikes designed to tempt nervous car drivers, born-again bikers with creaking joints and those with mobility or balance problems, out again 'into the wind' have been tried before. Who can forget the horrendous Ariel 3, or even the insanely dreadful Sinclair C5? None has tempted the 'real' biker. A brand-new product, the BRP Can-Am Spyder might succeed. This machine, like the Gilera and Piaggio, *does* have its twin wheels out front, in time-honoured Morgan fashion. Now (2009) being imported into the UK through Pump Action, the Spyder offers a very different experience from the two scooter-based three wheelers. Fitted with an Aprilia RSV Mille sports-bike engine reportedly giving 0-60mph in 4.5 seconds, Bosch stability control of brakes and traction and high quality of manufacture, it too might widen a market-place increasingly interested in safer ways of enjoying biking.

Differences between the UK and the USA, the home of the trike

In America, the bespoke trike builders have gone a lot further than their Brit cousins, and, in the most successful incarnations, have blended the front fender/trunk/engine part of the donor bike with matching fibre-glass bodywork over the rear wheels with integral seating and luggage compartment. The end result looks 100% factory-assembled with no overtones of kit-car or DIY bodge-up. These smooth lines have done a great deal to make trike ownership acceptable to a consumer-base that is acutely aware of form, as opposed to function. Such style has passed on to European trike manufacturers, notably the famous Dutch sidecar firm EML, whose impressively lovely Manhattan designs for

Passenger's eye view of a Boss Hoss trike's controls. Note the width of the gas tank with its car-like profusion of dials and those hyper-wide bars - certainly needed on a trike which retains telescopic forks and a huge front tyre. Sitting on one of these is like no other biking experience; the rounded contours, the plump expanses of metal, the vast weight, the rich throb of the V8, the whoosh of the 15" fan blade, the combination of quality metal and insane fantasy form have almost no counterpart!

The stunning Martin Conquest. This NABD-approved BMW 1150R conversion is designed to be driven from the wheelchair, which enters the trike from a rear ramp. Seat driven conversions are also available. (Photo courtesy of Martin-Conquest)

Harley-Davidson Tri-Glide trikes have to be the absolute last word in sophistication, marriage of the disparate parts and thus aesthetic satisfaction. These, luckily, are now (2009) imported into the UK through selected dealers (see *Sidecar and Trike Contacts*)

Part of the reason for this difference between US and UK trike styles has its origins in the laws appropriate to trike ownership in the two countries. In Britain, a trike is classed as a motorcycle if it weighs in under 410kg. For insurance, parking exemption and general use implications it is desirable to keep a trike light. This, in turn, means a fairly skeletal adaptation without the weight penalty of heavy, sweeping bodywork. Up to 450kg the vehicle is classed as a tricycle, losing some of the legal advantages of being a 'motorcycle' - like escaping city congestion charging, for example. Above 450kg the vehicle is technically a car, requiring car-like features to be fitted, such as hazard-warning lights and seat-belts on bench seats. Problems can crop up at the MoT test for these machines for which there isn't a clear definition in law. Keeping things light in the UK seems sensible, preferably under 410kg. At its lightest, incidentally (that is: not exceeding 254kg) the vehicle becomes 'an invalid-carriage for sole use of the rider'. And when a trike conversion consists merely of a bolted on rear-axle in place of the original single wheel, the vehicle is not subject to the Single Vehicle Approval (SVA) law in Britain.

An American alternative to a true trike: the outrigger support wheel

Before my examination of some American trikes - some of which are readily imported into Europe - it is worth touching upon a remarkable and uniquely American accessory. Should you wish to keep your bike stock and go as little a way as possible down the road of trike conversion, there are a couple of companies which manufacture bolt-on attachments to convert your bike from a two-wheeler to a form of four-wheeler, by using two support wheels on each side and continuing to use the bike's rear wheel for traction. The sprung 'outrigger' wheels are nicely-finished with wheel-trim, fenders and well-machined support parts. A modest frame attached to the motorcycle makes connections to the support wheels and these can be whisked off in a manner of minutes. As one of the firms puts it in its advertising: 'Go from Mild to Wild in moments'. The finished machine looks, at first glance, like a normal bike-donor trike - except that the outer wheels are of smaller diameter, and the main advantage of a trike is there: stability. Your bike is not hacked about, however, and can be resold as a solo without further attention. Tow-Pac has to be imported, but from 2008 Motorcycle Tour Voyager is available in the UK. As for their status in law, I believe that they rate as a simple sidecar does: an on/off bolt-on accessory which does not change the character of your machine from that of 'motorcycle'.

It is interesting how, every now and then, the idea of a covered trike or bike pops up, as in this big alien-looking and powerful motor-bicycle with electronic pop-up outrigger wheels from Switzerland, which caused a stir at Motorcycle World a few years back.

The Motorcycle Tour Voyager fits over 80 machines and makes no alterations to the original machine. Once your Voyager kit is on, you can zip it off in five minutes. The wheels adjust to corners and, unlike trike or sidecar conversions, being of negligible weight, add nothing to petrol consumption. The under-belly sub-frame robs the bike of over 1 inch clearance and might hit speed humps. Tow-Pac's 'Insta-Trike' has a U-frame round the bike's rear instead, but I've always thought that its original tiny 8 inch outrigger wheels look peculiar with a large bike. I've also wondered whether they might not suffer the risk of being run over by trucks coming up next to them in traffic because they are so very much below the bike's predominant sight outline. They now offer a much nicer 12 inch wheels option. Tow-Pac include a heavy duty hitch for trailer work.

Both are excellent ideas, however, and leave your valuable motorcycle unscathed at resale time. A recent company, Ghost Wheels, has come up with a variant on the theme, a fascinating concept which uses out-rigger wheels which pivot so that the bike can lean with them in corners, rather like the long-vanished bolt-on Sidewinders which acted as

Tiny Tow-Pac 'Insta-trike' quick-detach outrigger wheel-sets, here on a Honda GoldWing.

vestigial sidecars to enable British learner bikers to ride machines above 250cc, thirty years ago. These flexible *GhostWheels* versions of the 'Voyager' or 'Insta-Trike' do, however, like those ingenious adaptations, have three running tracks very close together, so would react quite a lot to the various striations and potholes of well-used modern roads. The twin-track of a sidecar machine definitely gives the comfier ride, because it's easier to straddle holes and humps. The fashion for square-section speed humps in Britain makes trike driving a slow affair in many suburban streets and plays havoc with machines which are too low-slung; another reason for opting for a bike-conversion with its short wheelbase and clearance, rather than a rear-engined VW one, in my opinion.

What to look for in the ideal commissioned trike

When you decide to have a motorcycle triked, it is useful to have at least some idea what your chosen manufacturer may do for you. There are certain things you should insist on, irrespective of blandishments to the contrary.

This German-manufactured Boom Fun III 500 automatic has a single cylinder fuel-injected 460cc motor with CVT automatic gearbox fitted to a Boom differential. This light, beautifully-finished trike is imported by Boom Trikes (UK) (Photo courtesy of Boom Trikes UK)

This style, offered in Europe by the Canadian firm of Lehman through its agents, takes a Suzuki Volusia and turns it into a neat, nippy scoot with top-class coachwork. This sort of machine has more practical appeal as something you might zip around on every day than a giant two litre behemoth - and it's cheaper on the gas. (Photo courtesy of Colin Appleyard Motorcycles Ltd.)

Left, not quite a trike, because two of its wheels are in-line, and not quite a sidecar outfit, this is a very rare 1923 Side-Motor, currently in the Verkehrshaus in Lucerne, Switzerland. The engine is mounted under the high passenger seat and drives both rear wheels deriving tractive power, presumably, from the weight of the person perched above. A narrow tracked vehicle is always desirable, but this seems much too narrow to make steering easy, although stability must be enhanced, even driven solo, by the engine's weight.

Below. If a really large, low, long trike capable of carrying three people at very high speeds (well over 100 mph) is what one must have, then a bike-conversion is unlikely to meet the need. What will do so is this, the Boom Fighter X12. With a 2 litre fuel-injected water-cooled engine coupled to a 5 speed gearbox and riding just a few inches off the ground on adjustable Konis and hefty leading-links, this machine – at nearly 4 metres in length and weighing in dry at 800 kgs, could be more satisfying than a Porsche (and nearly as expensive!) (Photo courtesy of Boom Trikes UK)

Your rear end

Obviously the trike has to be, above all, safe, so the quality of welded parts for the newly-applied rear end needs to be first class. The best trike shops use cold drawn seamless steel tubing, often of 2mm gauge and 1.25 inch diameter, and the welding is best done with a tungsten inert gas (TIG) welder using a jig to guarantee an accurate assembly. It is useful to be able to align for camber once the trike is put together, so enquire about a camber adjuster. Don't be happy with nameless after-market shock absorbers - the reputable firms use the best, like those from Hagon Products or Pro-Tech. Some trike shops use ex-Reliant axles, but more popular are Ford enclosed shaft differentials. If the hubs and brakes are also Ford, there is automatic peace of mind when it comes to spares and replacements. Sierra 2.0 prop-shafts and drive-shafts are a durable choice, as are Ford calipers and discs. Remember, although their products were once easy to get hold of, and cheaper, Reliant went out of business a fair time ago.

Trike builders will often offer a choice of chain, shaft or belt drive. I personally would go for shaft drive first, belt second and chain third - as I would with a solo bike. The arguments against prop shaft drive are based around the objections to a trike's main drawback: the large amount of unsprung weight relative to sprung weight. Obviously a shaft adds to this. The lightness of a bike conversion compared with the average car will make the axle and wheels a far greater proportion of the machine's total weight. This is likely to make the ride hard; indeed, the rear wheel-set may well tramp over ridged surfaces. This is a further argument against massive rear wheels and tyres, of course. However, the choice of dampers is the key. Hagons, for example, make a range which many builders use. As with sidecarring, what makes the ride sweetest is having either a plump passenger to settle the coil springs, or, failing that, discreetly applied lead. A trike's rear frame can have lead in several places - round the frame, under a bench seat or lining the trunk.

The best shops powder-coat these back ends, and although it may be tempting to go for yellow or silver, black is usually the sensible choice. In the long run it looks better too. Whatever you do, resist any attempt by your builder to leave off mud-guarding - it is a legal requirement for road use in the UK. Bare wheels are very often seen on show trikes, but these are not meant for real-world use. Skimpy, or worse, no mudguards are a pain in even light rain; the water flies up and is sucked onto you by the trike's passage. Insist on decent guards which come down to within 6 inch of the ground at the rear, and make sure they match the front one. It doesn't spoil things to ask your builder to put in a semi-circle of metal on the inner part of the guards; this will keep the diff and shafts much cleaner. Until you have had to do it, you can be unprepared for the bore of keeping

The choice of rear wheels here seems to err on the excessive, although this is a show trike and probably not expected to do serious mileage in all weathers. Those giant rubbers with no mudguards would make quite a splash. Note the large rear chain-wheel for low, low gearing from this modest Harley-Davidson Sportster. The underslung brake caliper, acting on a very small single disc, looks a little overwhelmed by its task. Generally each wheel needs to have its disc - as is usually the case with trike conversions using car axles. The biggest drawback of a set-up like this, however visually striking, is the amount of unsprung weight. The mounting of the axle, which has no differential, is concentrated within the narrow limits of the donor bike's original frame and thus there is little to absorb any but vertical motion. The solid alloys look great though, and note the sensible dodge of making the handlebar the same width as the track. This is definitely recommended on a single front wheel trike.

Horizontal spring/damper set up now nearly universal in trike design

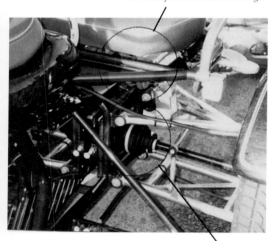

Left, an illustration of the amount of welded adaptation necessary to create a modern, fine handling trike from a solo bike. Note the workmanship and satisfying visibility of components. Covering them up with fibre-glass saves the inevitable cleaning, but then you worry about what's corroding under there!

Below. The Lehman solid axle, as fitted to all their trikes (imported into the UK by Colin Appleyard Motorcycles Ltd). The idea is that it is better to sacrifice the ride compliance of independently-sprung axles in order to enhance cornering. Certainly, these solid 'No-Lean' 3 wheelers corner without the body-sway and dipping that naturally occurs with independent drive shafts and wishbones. Here the big mono-shock can be seen next to the prop-shaft. (Photo courtesy of Colin Appleyard Ltd)

The universal joint taking drive from differential to rear wheels between the wish-bones

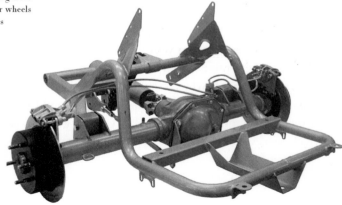

dirt and corrosion from a lot of exposed joints, mechanical parts and tubing. In a car, it's out of sight and out of mind, but the visible workings of a naked trike are part of its charm and they *have* to be clean.

The rear wheels are an important part of the vehicle. I would suggest that you avoid excessive width for reasons already touched on: noise, scrabbling, axle-tramp, water-splash. 6.5 x 15 inch wheels with 195/50/15 tyres are a good compromise, although 17 inch wheels don't go too far. It largely depends on the front end's wheel and stance. I do think that a skinny little front wheel and whacking great steam rollers at the back looks daft, and unsafe. Aesthetically, you should go for spokes all round, or alloy all-round, but not a mixture. There's no excuse not to get it right: there are dozens of wheel manufacturers and suppliers out there. Raceways of Donington, for example, stock Panther, Ultra, American Racing and Racelite wheels in every imaginable size. Racelite are British and make 15 inch wheels specially for the trike builder with diamond cut finish and drilled for Reliant, Ford, Jaguar and VW hubs.

Your front end

I am very much of the opinion that the front end of your bike should be left as stock as possible. There is a temptation to replace those forks with ones with a greater rake, but don't be too eager to get that stretched custom look on your trike. In a straight line you are stable, but bends become a challenge. On a bike, you can always lean into corners when your front wheel is way, way out there ahead of you. On a trike you steer, and both the perceived heaviness of steering and your lock-to-lock will be badly affected by too lengthy a rake. Again, what's okay on a show trike doesn't work so well on the street. You may consider leading-link forks, and firms such as Unit Sidecars make well-proven ones, but, while effective, they don't add much aesthetically. Your shrouded telescopics may look as good, or better, and simply need wider handle-bars to assist steering. I've seen several trikes with bars and mirrors which are virtually the same width as the machine's track, and that's a good idea. Quite a lot of your trike is outside your range of vision.

Your other rear end

Finally, my feeling is that your bike conversion should simply keep its existing saddle. On this you will have the commanding height of a motorcycle, your passenger can sit behind you as usual and you won't have the hassle of bench seating, seat-belts and racks, all of which look odd and spoil the pretty, homogeneous lines of your conversion.

The appeal of trikes is enormous, their road presence is terrific and they can be ridden without a helmet, if desired. The only drawback is that, if the conversion is done with commitment, it won't be worth trying to put the bike back to what it was; your trike will be for keeps and, in Britain for the present at least, resale will be into a tiny market.

Trike firms in the UK

The main UK firms currently operating - some of them with twenty years or more of award-winning designs under their belts, and most with websites - include those listed below. This list is by no means exhaustive, but contains the firms which advertise most widely and the details of which are usually found in the British custom bike magazines. They have websites with galleries of machines they have created and often a selection of new and used trikes for sale. As a guide, a complete second-hand bike-based trike would start at £10,000 and a stylish conversion of a new big cruiser (like a Triumph Rocket III or Harley-Davidson Road King) would be about £27,000. This is executive car money, so a top-flight trike is hardly a cheapo vehicle.

Baron Trikes supply fibre-glass bodies for H/D, Honda and Victory

BB Customs of Ferndown, Dorset, specialists in Harley conversions

Boom Trikes (UK), Manchester, imports the whole range of offerings from German company, Boom Trikes. These run from single cylindered automatic vehicles, through V-Twin to Ford Focus power

C&C Trikes of Maidstone, Kent, will create a vehicle from any shaft-driven bike

Colin Appleyard Motorcycles of Keighley, West Yorkshire, are agents for the EML Manhattan conversions for Harleys and for Lehman products

Custom Works of Langley Mill, Nottinghamshire has built show-winning machines and will make one-off bits as required

Eurotech Engineering of Colliers Green, Kent, build anything from custom to speed record breakers

Harley Davidson dealers supply, from 2009, their Tri-Glide trike

Lightning Custom of Binbrook, Lincs, make to customer specifications

MBT Customs supplies Rewaco rear-engined trikes in several guises, with motors from VWs, Harleys and the Ford Zetec 16

Metal Magic convert or bespoke build trikes

Pro-Custom of Rotherham, South Yorkshire make, as the name suggests, custom trikes

Rhino Trikes in Somerset bases part of its range on Suzuki 'Intruder' cruisers - and very well-suited to triking these bikes are; better than solos really because their handling never quite matched their lovely 1400cc engines

TAB Customs of Doncaster, have specialised in DragStar conversions

The Trike Shop of Cardiff, South Wales. This well-known, and one of the oldest established manufacturers in the UK, uses Ford parts (which makes the spares situation easy) and offers choices of belt-, chain- or shaft-drive

Trike Design of Caerphilly, Wales (Hank's Chop Shop) is known to be inventive and flexible and has made some very well-sorted designs. Currently imports the Dutch EML design for Harley 'Road King' models, and has a franchise for Lehman's Harley trikes

Trikes UK of Bolton in Lancashire imports Boom Trikes from Germany and also sells the Ural Wolf trike. Boom are VW air-cooled and Ford engined, car-derived designs

Ultra Cycles is a spin-off of Ural Motoworld and adds a third wheel to the rugged 750cc boxer twin from Russia. These trikes look a lot better now than they did a few years ago, for some reason

United Trikes of Abbotskerswell, Newton Abbott, Devon make a neat rear axle and suspension system for converting a bike to a trike

V12 Trikes of Carmarthen, Wales, import Lehman Trikes

A Wildcat trike made by Chris Spalding Engineering. This, their only model, is based round the Rover 114 automatic with the 'K' series all-aluminium 1400cc ohc four-cylinder liquid-cooled motor and CVT automatic gearbox with reverse and kickdown. The cold-drawn frame is supported by Yamaha TDM forks and, at the rear, a mixture of Rover and Wildcat's components: a double wishbone with hydrogas units. (Photo courtesy of Chris Spalding Engineering)

Wackey's Trikes, another Devon firm, this time from Okehampton has the capacity for creating virtually anything - as long as you can pay for it. There is something very appealing about this firm's design of rear mudguard, which has a pleasantly 'deco' nacelle containing the sidelights and indicators

Wildcat Trikes in Lincolnshire are unusual in offering a Rover 114 automatic 'K' series powered machine with all-encompassing bodywork

US trike manufacturers: after all, you could import one...

Although it is slowly changing in the UK - amazingly, there were a couple of glitzy trikes in the Lord Mayor of London's Show procession in 2006 - the true home of triking is America. It is perfectly possible to ship over a completed machine from the USA to Europe (but not cheap) and the range of what is available is fascinating. Most of the trike makers offer anything from bare-frame kits to fully road-ready vehicles and the finished quality of American trikes is always first-class.

Better'n'Most Trikes which takes a stock bike and puts a transaxle in place of the rear wheel, Brit-style. It's a bit homely, but simple and stable.

Boss Hoss looms over most with vast, completely mad trikes of almost edibly delightful styling. They offer several styles of car back: '50s wings or rounded rump and also a truck. Their narrow Ford 8.8 rear differential and high boot, which perfectly complements that huge tank and engine, makes a trike which would stop a multitude fleeing from a lava-flow in its tracks. It is, if sanity tottered on its throne and all sense of planetary responsibility fled, what I would plump for, that is if I didn't get hold of an EML Manhattan conversion on a Harley Road King. It's the cobby shape and completeness of the *tout ensemble* of both of these that seduces, I suppose.

A Boss Hoss trike at the Ace Cafe, London - a rare monster in the UK. The vast size of the superstructure almost makes the Chevy V-8 big block look like a normal motorcycle engine. This example seemed all the larger for being painted bright yellow.

California Sidecar Inc make GoldWing and Valkyrie trike conversions as well as Harleys. They give a lot of attention to good looks so that bike and rear axle blend as if designed that way originally.

Champion Sidecars produce a Honda GL1800 kit for home assembly and this company also has good lines which blend the rear axle into the bike.

DFT Kits include handsome trunk and wheel-trim and make pleasant conversions of big Hondas.

Ecstasy Cycles Corp market the bizarre 'Renegade' line. These are more like custom cars with a single front wheel.

Hannigan Sidecar Co have kits for converting the big BMW K1200s to a trike

Kopavi Trikes are as long as a Bentley and stunning to look at. The Chevrolet V8 ensures that for a start, and the body-work is gorgeous. But imagine trying to find a parking space in London or Paris for one! They are not cheap, either.

Lehman are arguably North America's premier trike manufacturers, started modestly by John Lehman, who built a trike for his wife, Linda, but now a publicly traded company based in a 53,000sq ft factory in Alberta, Canada. Their 'Renegade' model is compact and Harley-based with beautiful bodywork. Lehman are one of the few trans-Atlantic manufacturers whose products are imported fairly widely into Europe, mainly the Monarch II built around the Honda Goldwing.

Motor Trike like Lehman, breaks away from the near-universal adaptation of the Honda 'GoldWing' and offer some small machines: the first based on the Suzuki 'Volusia' and the second on the Honda 'Shadow'. Does one need much more than 750cc on a nice, nifty little unit which parks easily, turns on itself and is economical to run and insure?

Novatrikes try to maintain a traditional motorbike look with big fuel tank, dual seat and bodywork covering that gaping space where the engine should be, but they too rely on VW power from reconditioned motors, and the mixture of the two styles doesn't quite convince.

Tri-King Trikes (no relation to the old UK firm which produced Morgan-style runabouts) produces trikes which boast an automatic levelling system using sprung air which, they claim, gives the comfiest ride of any trike.

Tri-Wing Industries Corp in Canada makes conversions for the magnificent Yamaha 'Venture Royale' and XVS1100 with typical well-made plastic bodywork.

The Vigillante Corporation makes a full-bodied mini-car trike with a small-block Chevrolet engine. Although its layout is reminiscent of a Reliant Robin on steroids, its low weight (under 720kg) and its 700bhp motor give it the power-to-weight ratio of a Formula 1 racing car. It is strangely appealing, if utterly bonkers.

WHICH SIDECAR FOR YOUR BIKE?

Although I have written of the seductive charms of triking, on balance I find sidecarring more appealing. It's partly to do with familiarity - I'm very used to having a shape flitting along on my left-hand side; it comes naturally to manoeuvre from one side of a vehicle because, of course, one does that in a car. I'm less used to the knowledge that there are two sticking-out things on each side behind my range of vision. Also, if you are going to encumber your solo with wheel number 3, you might as well make it useful for luggage-carrying/fetching shopping/holding wet-weather gear and tools and all that. With a non-booted, bare-axle, Brit-style trike you still end up with no more carrying capacity than a solo. Then, if you have only one bike, there's the matter of reversion to solo use - often necessary at major service time if you want a bike dealer to fit your machine through his narrow workshop doorway. Reversion is fairly easily done with most chairs, even when you've added leading-link forks or made suspension and gearing changes.

I bumped into a singularly contented man not long ago in a London suburban car park. He was collecting his grandson from primary school. The child was being fitted into a natty miniature helmet and his mode of transport home to tea was a well-used MZ bike and Velorex sidecar. The machine was unpretentiously oily, with a fair amount of scuffs, rust and sunshine-fading of its paint. The sidecar had bright homemade wiring skating all around its frame to the lights on its mudguard. It also had an obviously retro-fitted, but well-made, welded roll-over bar. At its rear was a tow hook. It was attached to its MZ (registered some eleven years previously) with three-point fixings, for this bike lacks a cradle frame.

Its owner told me that he and family had recently taken it 100 miles to Wiltshire on a camping holiday, towing their equipment in a trailer. "It took ages," said he, smiling self-deprecatingly at the memory, "all day, in fact. But then I can't get more than 45mph out of the outfit when it's fully loaded." I was amazed. I should have thought 20mph would have been more likely. We were, after all, talking about a 250cc two-stroke single. "I find the whole thing really useful for going to the rubbish dump - or collecting children," he added with a twinkle. He was well-spoken, grey-bearded, very casually dressed; he might have been a poet or retired lecturer in Ancient History. He was, perhaps, the ideal sidecar man: non-conformist, fond of the patina of a hard-worked hack, simple in his tastes, amusedly aloof from the driven insecurities and the design-led belief in the importance of appearances which characterise twenty-first century life.

Obviously, most people aren't like him; I'm not. Design, shape, feel, ethos all mean too much to most people - especially where their wheels are concerned - but what that faded, oily, home-painted, hard-slogged outfit told me was: don't worry, just do it. Decide on a chair, sling it on and just enjoy it. Ironically, by the way, the self-effacing, wry persona of my possibly retired poet was at odds with the interest his bizarre (to modern eyes) vehicle provoked. A new four-cylinder Kawasaki race replica was parked next to the MZ outfit and no one gave it a second glance.

So, should you have the urge to run something alongside your bike, what should that something be? Armed with the comforting thought that any recently-built motorcycle can, within reason, cope with hauling a sidecar, and assuming that you probably possess a bike which, in the recent past, would have been thought a large-capacity one (ie: over 500cc), I thought I might start with some thoughts on fixing the sidecar to the motorcycle. Then I am going to take a look at the sidecars themselves, starting with the larger ones and working my way through to the smaller and more outlandish designs.

Fixing the sidecar to the bike

Up until about 1962, the larger manufacturers of motorcycles in Britain - and that, at the time, meant the major motorcycles in use in the world - built a sidecar lug of some sort into the frames of nearly all machines of 500cc or over. This generally took the form of a circle of metal just under the head-stock, standing proud of the down-tube. Into it went the horizontal end of a metal bar called a 'swan-neck' - a sort of inverted J - the fitment at the lower vertical end attaching to a substantial clamp at the front of the sidecar frame. This made a rigid connection at one point. Sometimes this circular lug was matched by another just below the saddle which took a massive bolt with U-clamp mated to a strut at the back end of the chair's frame. Some manufacturers, like BMW, provided a ball or two, ready to take a rose pinch joint at fore or aft along the bottom of the bike's frame. The rest of the attachments were expected to be clamps, and adjustments to achieve the happiest alignment of bike and chair were handled by these clamps which slid up and down, or along the perimeter tubing of the bike frame.

Left. The 'swan-neck' and assorted massive ironmongery attaching this BMW to a Palma. Right. The straight arms and U-bolts going to welded ears attaching this Unit Sprite to its Yamaha. In neither case is that scenario of old comedy films - the sidecar coming off - in the least likely.

After the advent of the British Motor Corporation's 'Mini', and other small cars, which rendered the sidecar obsolete within ten years, bike makers ceased to provide cast-in lugs or balls. From the 1970s onwards, sidecars were often attached by clamps alone. Many sidecar pilots, myself included, disliked this arrangement. Clamps, unless a perfect fit, can bite into frame tubes and distort them; they always ruin the paint and leave marks, and they tend to lose alignment and slide around in use, especially on bumpy roads.

The aesthetic problem of clamps

The design of these has not changed since the 1950s or earlier, and swan necks, tube-clamps and sections of tubing intended to slide are the commonest methods of marrying chairs to bikes with conventional frames. While a period feel is guaranteed, it does not make for a pretty connection. Sometimes I've seen 100% clamped connections with a quite bizarre relationship between swan-neck, head-stock and chair, to say nothing of the lower tie-up. No doubt these were cobbled together by their owners, but the mixture of rusty hunks of over-sized ironmongery and spindly, frail tubes on some of these period combos, look unsafe as well as hideous.

The odds-and-sods method of creating an outfit - a clamp at one angle here, a through-bolt there, another clamp on a short tube leading to another clamp on a longer tube leading to a further clamp jammed up against a battery cover - makes three things very awkward: adjustment, removal and refit. Adjustment with such a set-up is guaranteed to be needed every now and then. You don't notice at first, but the steering seems increasingly heavy to the right, or there are squeaks and groans over road-humps, or the bike seems to be leaning affectionately towards its chair - and, hey-presto, all those clamps need slackening off, the soft-headed mallet has to come out and the bike and sidecar banged back into a happy union again. This union, incidentally, is not entirely governed by 'feel' on the road - although that is by far the most important consideration, assuming you know how well a sweetly-aligned outfit can drive - but by parameters established in the earliest years of sidecarring.

Toe-in and lean-out

Most bikers used to know about this forty years ago, but as outfits have become rarer, so the knowledge has grown a little more arcane. The bike should lean-out about an inch from the chair, measured by a bob-line from the handle-bars near the centre-line. This is because the sidecar wheel will spend a fair amount of its life down the road camber. The bike will run in a straight line if upright when nearer the crown of the road. Because the chair's weight is to one side, the straight-line running will also be helped if the chair's nose has a bit of 'toe-in' - perhaps an inch or two. Too much will cause scuffing of the sidecar tyre, too little will have the effect of pulling the bike into the sidecar when running under slight acceleration. This particular adjustment really does depend on rider 'feel'. When it is right, you'll know it. Finally, the sidecar's wheel axle should run about 6 to 9 inches ahead of the bike's rear spindle. This helps steering away from the chair. Each of these little parameters is variable and should be based on experiment in operation. It is not always true that a professionally done set-up is absolutely right for you, by the way. I've never left my combo just as it has been fitted for me. If, for example, you drive a great deal in town, a 'country lane' lean-out of bike may be too much. Your chair-wheel is less often in the camber because of parked cars. Similarly, if you almost never take a passenger in the chair, you can find that toe-in designed for this contingency is a little too much and the bike tends to pull into the sidecar.

All this fiddling is quite fun. It smacks of big boy's Meccano. But it can be tiresome if the connections are clunky, rusty and obdurate. Much more irritating is the difficulty of whipping the chair on and off, especially single-handed, when all the connections are at different angles to each other and the whole lot has to be re-aligned every time.

Many modern manufacturers have overcome many of these problems by using specially produced sub-frames and quickly detachable mountings. The set up of bike and sidecar can be easily altered and removing and refitting the sidecar made much easier. Of course, some manufacturers such as Watsonian tend to favour the traditional clamp mountings whilst others, such as Unit, have a rather more sophisticated approach. Which is best for your bike and sidecar will depend a little on personal preference and mostly on which sidecar you intend to fit to which bike.

Removing your chair for the bike's service

There are those whose sidecar and bike never take a break from wedded bliss (or hell). If you have fitted special leading-link forks and flat car-type tyres, or have removed your side-stand so that your bike can't be used as a solo again, there may be problems in some servicing centres. I've found that almost no bike garages like catering for outfits: their approaches are too narrow, or their workshops depend on hoisting the solo bike up on a bench, or they need the space. If you use one of them, you'll have to take your chair off for service. Clearly, it would be nice (and cheaper) to do everything at home; if you had a garage, a bench, the right tools, the know-how, the workshop manual and the time. But a lot of modern machines depend on a computer link-up, on diagnostic gear and specialised manufacturer knowledge and with them it's best not to tinker. Nowadays - perhaps it was always so - the most reliable bikes are those which are left well alone.

When, therefore, you need to take your chair off - either to use your bike as a solo, or to take it for servicing - you want the operation to go easily. There is nothing more obdurate and perverse than a sidecar without its bike. It is extremely difficult to manhandle on its one wheel, and the heavier it is, the more maddening is the task. It needs, therefore, to slip in one motion from its fitments, coming to rest on tough foam supports, and to go back from this position.

If you like to return your bike to solo use now and then, your sidecar should come off easily, preferably single-handedly. There is no doubt it is handier if you have straight armed fittings which bolt onto reachable lugs, and sturdy blocks of foam to support the sidecar as you wheel your bike away.

Large two/three seaters: a dying breed

The biggest chair currently on offer in the UK is the Oxford 3-4 seater made in Gloucestershire by Watsonian-Squire. This firm, almost certainly the oldest manufacturer of sidecars in the world, was started in 1911 by Frederick Watson of Conybere Street, Birmingham, England. In the earliest days of motor vehicle usage it was illegal to park anywhere on the roadway, especially at night - a state of affairs which persisted until quite recent days. An article about the law in a mid-'60s *Motorcycle and Three-wheeler Mechanics* made just this point to a reader who asked about it - parking was allowed by grace and favour of the local council and the police because of increased car ownership. It's a reminder of the current staggering ownership figures in Britain (currently in excess of 30,000,000) that many sidewalks have been over-painted with white lines to permit a street of cars to mount the kerb and park on half of the pavement's width.

In Fred Watson's day, it was expected that you would tuck your bike up the alley beside your house, or even in the house's hallway. With a sidecar attached, this became impossible. Watson's answer was to create a collapsible chair which folded up against the bike and could fit through a door. Later, by 1920, his firm manufactured a quick-release sidecar, the body of which attached by four wing-nuts to a frame on the bike. This frame stayed fixed in place, even when the bike was used as a solo. A small castor-wheel under the chair body helped with the task of wheeling the thing away. Frederick Watson originally named his company The Collapsible Sidecar Co, but had the sense to see that this conjured up alarming images. By 1913 he had coined the name 'Watsonian'. In 1988 Squire sidecars acquired the old firm and its designs and now offers both its own sidecars and some of Watsonian's classic 1960s fibre-glass bodies.

For nearly fifty years the sidecar body has, most commonly, been made of glass-fibre: ideal, strong and so much more long-lasting than the wood and steel, leather-cloth

The capacious and stately Watsonian Oxford with matching trailer. You need a big motorcycle to haul four people and their luggage and camping gear. Dwarfed by the sidecar is a BMW K100 'flying-brick' - I think. Note the countries to which this combo has travelled.

A 1960s single trying to peak out from behind the streamlined bulk of a Busmar Astral, coach built from wood and aluminium. This chair makes an intersting comparison with the modern Oxford (see previous page). The Busmar attempts to be a lot more car like whilst the new chair is pure unreconstructed sidecar - a confident and unashamedly different mode of transport.

or aluminium-clad creations of the fifty years before that. All Watsonian-Squire's models are now of this material.

In the early 1960s Watsonian introduced a wrap-round perimeter tube chassis known as the 'Silk chassis'. This had a small 10 inch wheel and short, damped-link suspension. This is what underpins the big Oxford and Cambridge chairs of today - in wider, longer form. Although you may wish to transport a family of four or five on your outfit, it's more likely that the purchase of such a large chair is to carry camping gear on tour, or, just as viable, to complement the lines of a really big bike. If you possess a hefty GoldWing, you can all too easily end up with the motorcycle dominating a too low and narrow chair.

The vast family sidecars of the late 50s and early 60s, such as Canterbury's Carmobile or Busmar's Astral are, naturally, no longer made. They absolutely overwhelmed the small 600cc singles and 650cc twins that were all that were available to hitch them to. Even the rare Ariel Square Four one-litre machines, which many thought were ideal for family sidecar haulage, were not built around frames much bigger than standard 500s. Really, such big sidecars were constructed out of their era and needed a Boss Hoss or GoldWing to get them down to size!

A firm run by Fred Yates made the Gemini in the '80s - a lower, less successfully eye-catching version of the '60s behemoths, and, if desperate for a whiff of rolling *nostalgie*, one might find one for sale second-hand. However, as I have implied, virtually the only current choice for a three-seat chair on either side of the Atlantic is a Watsonian. They do

You need to choose carefully. Nowadays , some really
big bikes (like this Honda Aspencade) dominate
quite large sidecars, as is the case with this flat
front, 10 inch wheeled, Watsonian Palma.

have their drawbacks, though. Although their width is very reassuring at all times and
you never feel that the wheel will lift on left hand corners, nor that car drivers will try to
harry you out of their way, they do require a fair amount of horse-power and torque to
pull, noise levels are loud within, the ride is lively and the all-fabric roof is too low, with
its fiddly poppers able only to be attached from outside. Those huge saloon chairs of the
past had proper hinged doors; the Oxford has to be climbed into, even though the window
scuttle can be lifted up to make entry easier. These sidecars come in various permutations
of wheel/mudguard design and can be colour-matched.

The nearest thing to these in road-presence is Squire's own RX4, a side-by-side
two-seater which perfectly complements a large cruiser. This chair looks stylish around
the roof-line and the wheel assembly integrated into the body is pleasantly modern.

The Squire RX4 on a sports tourer which has been
adapted with leading-link forks, flat section car tyres
and steering damper. (Photo: Watsonian Squire)

Low light sports chairs across the decades. Above is a super comfy 1950s Steib with sprung body. Note the long springs at the sides. The hammock style seat was also comfortable - if you could get into it. The flexible windscreen surround provided no hand-holds and stepping onto the plush upholstery was inevitable.

Below is the author's Unit Hedingham Sprite, manufactured half a century later - still with flexible screen providing no support and requiring the passenger to step on the seat in order to get in. In both cases form supercedes function.

The only other current giants are those from the Dutch firm of EML, but, like the large Tremola made by Armec, are not found in right-hand drive form. Such a pity, this British custom of driving on the left, because for some years now it has been against UK law to pilot an outfit with the chair on the 'wrong' side. I spoke to a most amusing chap at a rally recently who drove a Ural with driven side-car wheel, fitted to the right of the bike. He told me that it was his personal two-fingered gesture to "those lying bastards in the government". He also told me that the police had never actually stopped him. It is an illogical law, because no such ruling prohibits a left-hand drive car being used on British roads.

Opinions used to differ about whether it was useful to have a totally enclosed saloon-bodied sidecar or an open one with occasional hood, like an old MG sports car. There was a vogue for saloons on both sides of the Atlantic, though they became entrenched in Britain, probably because of the cool, damp weather of fifty years ago. Most were sheet-metal / wood affairs with canvas-duck roofs. Watsonian made the latest incarnation of its Ascot in the same manner as the PMB (Plastic Motor Bodies) - a totally enclosed plastic saloon with car-like doors and windows and wheel housed within the bodyline. Both were too expensive and too late. A few firms persisted with this sort of design, like Martello Sidecars of Kent and also Squire until quite recently, but such models were, and are, rare.

The more common sports sidecar

The single-seater sports design - low, with raked windscreen, tonneau and occasional hood - has become the norm, especially, as I have already suggested, because fewer people actually travel in them, outside occasional leisure use, and they are seen as attractive embellishments of the motorcycle in their own right.

There is a surprisingly big choice of these in the UK at the time of writing and a growing choice in America. Nearly all of them are medium to small size single seaters. Some advertise themselves as 'child-adult', which simply means that they have a 26 inch wide seat instead of an 18 inch one. The vogue for rows of seats behind each other has virtually gone (except in the giant Watsonian Oxford).

Ever since the heyday of the sports designs of the 1930s, form has taken precedence over function. Whereas saloon chairs had doors ahead of the single wheel, 'real' sports sidecars never featured any opening bodywork. The passenger has to step over the mudguard, put a leg into the cockpit, stand on the seat and lower himself or herself into the abyss. While getting in is difficult, getting out is worse - especially for the plump or creaky. Once the legs are stretched out into the nose, it's a tussle against the force of gravity that had assisted one to get in. The ancient and iconic Steibs of the '50s demanded this sort of gymnastics, as did their English copies by Garrard and Watsonian; so did the Wessex, the Canterbury Arrow and the Blacknell Gran Strada. The Unit Hedinghams, Velorexes and small Armecs of today are no different.

I do try at least once to sit in each sidecar that I buy, but I was nearly trapped forever in my latest: the pretty, but intractably low and petite Unit Sprite. The ease with which one plumps down into the depths of a sports chair of this type is ample illustration of Newton's dictum that all falling bodies are being pulled relentlessly towards the centre of the earth. Pulling oneself away again from the prone position, without rails to hold on to, straps or rocket-assistance is another matter.

Chairs you can get into easily - military dinosaurs, trials and lifting scuttles

Three exceptions to this common design are still obtainable. The first is the Russian Ural sidecar - a copy of the WWII Steib used in *blitzkrieg*. This has a large cut-out into which one can step, ahead of the wheel, and it's not too low, thanks to a 19 inch wheel and the mounting of the stub axle below the body. Drawbacks are the howling gales in motion. The exposed seating position is most useful if peering through the sights of an attached machine-gun. The second is Unit's ETH, made originally for the new generation BMW Boxers. This is like a tall 'trials' chair - a sort of exposed seat at hip height on a platform with a flat nose-panel ahead of it. It can be just walked into. It's pleasant being on the same level as the driver, but again you do feel exposed to the elements. It looks strange too. The third design is that used for Watsonian's Palma, RX4 and Oxford models and for several of the sidecars from EZS and EML in Holland. These chairs are quite low, but they have a lifting windscreen and scuttle which make entry and egress a little bit easier but the emphasis is generally on the word 'little'.

But really the practicality of ingress and exit from a chair has never been high on the rider's list - after all, the rider, by definition, never travels in it. What matters is the look of the ensemble and its handling.

Before I go on to discuss the details of the range of sports chairs on the market, I must add a word or two more about the point that the rider never has a spin in his own sidecar. While true 99.99% of the time, the existence of one or two preserved 'SEALS' does give evidence that it was once considered a good idea for rider and passenger to travel, not separated, but together, side-by-side. The SEAL (an acronym for Sociable, Economical And Light) was manufactured in Manchester, England between 1912 and 1930. The designers had the astonishing lateral notion of putting all accommodation in the sidecar, over its one wheel, and leaving a saddle-less, rider-less motorcycle outside, bolted on and controlled by wires, doing the work. I really like the surreal image of a little 1920s family of three snug in the sidecar under cover while a ghostly, untenanted bike roars away beside them in the rain and the dark. The National Motorcycle Museum has a fascinating preserved SEAL in its collection.

One you can get into, the military style Ural. (Photo courtesy F2 Motorcycles)

The surreal SEAL in the National Motorcycle Museum.

It is rather extraordinary that the choice of small to medium chairs is as good now as it has ever been since the early '60s. Quite why this should be so, I don't know, because the demand for them must be modest - if that invisibility on our roads, which I've already alluded to, is anything to go by. Of course, very few of them are bought for utilitarian purposes, so the market dictates a wide choice for a self-indulgent, individualistic purchase. That's capitalism for you. In the old USSR there were only two styles, and yet they could be seen everywhere.

What follows next is a quick review of what models of sidecar are available on the UK, European and US market but the emphasis is on the UK. I've included the details of a few American chairs because they have some fascinating refinements largely unknown in Britain. I thought I'd split this review into two parts: rigid sidecars and leaners. This is because, although one never sees them in the UK, there is a vogue elsewhere in the world for bikes that lean with sidecars that don't, and bikes and sidecars that lean together. There is no substitute for seeing these models in the flesh, so to speak, and the main sidecar gatherings - like Sidecar Saturday at the Ace Café, London - and the owners' club meetings throughout the year, provide opportunities to study combinations close up and to look at the designs I am going to whiz quickly through now.

Leaning chairs and leaning bikes: a European phenomenon

Up to now, all the chairs I have discussed have been rigid designs - that is to say the chair and bike are intended to be a single unit, each part incapable of independent movement from the other. This certainly seems to be the favoured method of fitment in the UK. In the USA, and on the European mainland, there is a fondness for the flexible combination, but it has never caught on in Britain.

There are two types of leaning bikes and chairs: one in which both bike and chair lean on corners together, the sidecar supported on a tiny wheel amidships, and the other in which the bike leans and the sidecar and its frame remain uncannily horizontal to the road. Watsonian-Squire was the manufacturer who brought the former, the Anglo-Dutch Flexit, to the UK in 1992. Armec still construct the latter in Switzerland. Each of these is a fascinating device, but each has one drawback: unsupported, even though there is friction in the leaning systems, the bike can flop sideways, not just when stationary, but when being ridden very slowly - as when manoeuvring into parking spaces. The Flexit had a locking lever to hold bike and chair in rigid relationship, but one had to remember to use it, and it required the rider to put a foot down to steady things as with a solo. The Flexit linkage is handled by chains within the chassis tubes and greased points, the Armec's by pivoted joints low down beneath the motorcycle's frame - and the sensations of each are sufficiently strange for their relative scarcity to be understandable.

When each combo is working well, when the road surface is not exacerbating the effect of the Flexit's tiny 10 inch central wheel and when the vast distance between the Armec and its tug (necessary for the bike to have room to lean over the chair) is not affecting steering and pull — there is considerable exhilaration in being able to lean again in corners as if on a solo. It is what a bike does best, sweeping without loss of speed, side to side, round the curves. To see and feel the entire Flexit combo hunkering into the turn

The remarkable Flexit, a Dutch tilting sidecar design offered a few years ago in the UK by Watsonian-Squire, here seen fitted to a Honda Gold Wing (Photo: Watsonian-Squire)

Right. Similar designs can be found on offer in America too. This fuzzy picture was obtained from a US website (but which I now can't trace, so I apologise for reproducing it without permission) but it shows very well the unconventional stance of these leaning chairs and their relative smallness.

Below: shark nosed, single-seat Swiss Armec on a Moto Guzzi 850cc Le Mans transverse V-twin

with you, like a high speed tilting train, is to experience sidecarring without effort with no need to use the handlebars as a tiller. The passenger, cocooned above the fat little wheel in a plastic space-ship, must also find this negation of gravitational force a boon (even if part of his or her mind must be wondering if those chains really are going to take the strain and stay intact). Quite what a passenger feels in the Armec sidecar, which stays bolt upright as the plot whistles round curves, I can't say, having never ridden in one, but, as 300kg of Harley-Davidson or BMW 1200 suddenly keels overhead, he or she must also hope that those linkages are both well-greased and tightened sufficiently.

The Armec chair is at least open, so, in theory, one could escape if the worst happened; the Flexit has an electrically-operated window/roof which seals the trusting passenger in, absolutely cut off from bike, its pilot and the open air.

Watsonian-Squire marketed the Flexit for a short time in Britain, but it didn't seem to catch on and the only ones I've ever come across have been fitted on the right-hand side for Continental riding - and some of these looked slightly different from the Flexit depicted in the catalogues, so I imagine they were competing designs. Their scarcity on the home market would make it difficult to obtain one for left-hand drive. What with that, and with a seemingly ingrained British fondness for rigid mounting, we are unlikely to see many, if any, on our roads.

UK sidecar manufacturers and importers

Charnwood Classic Restorations

Charnwood has made a name for itself with chairs for high-performance machines, but has also made a light, attractive chair called the Meteor in both single seat and one-and-a half seat versions for a few years now. It uses the chassis on which Watsonian bases the Stratford and its body is modelled on a WWII aircraft drop-tank - these being pressed into use as sidecars after 1945. It has the nice art-deco pointy rear of the UNIT Sprite, but has a more 'period' bulbous nose. The windscreen of the single-seater is also a period device: a pane of glass held in a metal frame by aluminium knurled nuts. This looks good, but doesn't do a lot to keep off the elements. The wider version has a standard Perspex screen. I don't think the shape of either is perfectly complemented by the Watsonian mudguard, but it is good value and charismatic and, although the smaller one in particular is designed for medium-sized bikes, both look perfectly at home on larger ones.

Charnwood are, as I've said, as well known in sidecar circles for their own remarkable sports chairs, designed by Jim D'Arcy and originally fitted to very high-powered BMW K1 and Japanese sports bikes and designed to be at ease at well over the UK's 70mph

Charnwood can supply their own Meteor
sidecar fitted to a modern Royal Enfield
Bullet. Their ribbed piped seat is very
attractive, as is the simple Watsonian
chassis with its Jubilee mudguard and
16 inch spoked wheel. The glamorous
'antique aircraft' style of windscreen is
not particularly effective, but - in
common with other aspects of the chair
- form here outvotes the utilitarian.
Charnwood are also the place to go if
you are after a genuine old chair (like
this pre-war saloon) - a jolly car based
design with windows all of 8 inches deep.
Charnwood often have a selection of old
chairs in stock.

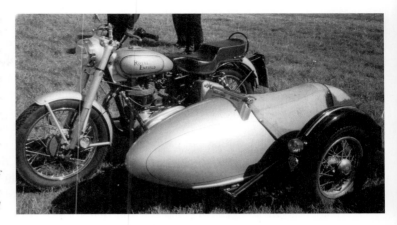

limit. These chairs are strikingly coloured and wind-cutting, with the latest alloy wheels
and powerful brakes. A roll-over bar is built-in, a spoiler is fitted under the nose and
the mudguard runs up from a stream-lined point to a handsome mounting of lights.
The seat is high-backed and plushly padded. These chairs are designed to be permanently
attached to their motorcycles which themselves will have been the subject of
considerable modification; at the very least fitted with leading-link forks and lowered
gearing and car tyres. The outfits brought into existence in this way are not cheap but
raise the use of a sidecar on public roads to a level undreamt of in the sidecar's heyday.
I have alluded earlier to the impact one of these 'aggressive plots' made on a journalist
in a review for *Motorcycle Sport and Leisure* in 1999. Charnwood also sell and fit second-
hand and new chassis and bodies from other makers from their premises in Coalville,
Leicester, where a selection can be viewed. There was a suggestion that the firm was
going to change hands not long ago, but at the time of writing (2008) it is actively
advertising in the motorcycle press, as usual.

Merlin Sidecars

Merlin Sidecars come from the wonderfully named town of Pity Me, Durham, and go a long way down the path of creating a single unit out of a bike and chair. They make two models: the Super Sport which can be seen on machines as diverse as a 500cc scooter and high-powered race reps and which all seem to have glaring eye logos on their noses, and the F11 - a flowingly organic 'bat mobile' of a chair. These breath-taking Formula 1 car style combos blend motorcycle and sidecar into all-encompassing bodywork, filling the gap between them. The sheer volume of fibre-glass looks enormous, largely because it is all so low down. I've not yet seen an F11 Merlin adaptation which does not have small car-wheels for the bike (to lower the gearing and provide vivid acceleration) and all sorts of suspension, braking and suspension tweaks. Triumph triples seem to be popular with Merlin types. This fashion for racing-car expanses of bodywork across the constituent parts is more commonly seen abroad than in the UK, particularly in Germany where such unifying is practised by several firms. Merlin combinations are rare, but once seen are not forgotten. Generally their owners favour eye-popping graphics such as flares, bursts of contrasting colours,

Eye-popping Merlin F11 chairs on Triumph and Suzuki Sports tourers. These are the nearest thing to a racing outfit on the road. The grille on the right-hand combo is a 'trompe l'oeil' painting - but it looks real enough to be the air intake to a vast V8 motor.

painted-on 'grilles' suggestive of the cooling required for vast engines, and the wizard logo of Merlin themselves. A row of two or three of these at a bike show makes as big an impact as if a group of flying saucers had landed.

Warwick Sidecars

The ephemeral and individual nature of the sidecar industry is quite well illustrated by Warwick Sidecars whose website I once found and whose product seemed to be a handsome EML-ish chair of attractive dimensions. Further searches have come up with nothing, however - and I've not spoken to anyone who has seen one.

Watsonian-Squire

Watsonian-Squire has a good number of models available: The Squire RX4, ST3, PV1 and ML1 and the Watsonian Stratford, Manx, Monza, Monaco Palma and GP Jubilee, nearly all of these with different trim levels and wheel sizes.

The ST3 is much liked because it is light, modern-looking and strong. Its style is particularly apt on modern, naked or faired touring machines of medium capacity, and it rides well on its alloy wheel. It looks best with the hood off, its roll-bar and high-backed seat giving it a sort of off-road, competitive flavour. The windscreen tilts forward to make entry and exit easier. Luggage can be stored behind the seat and on aluminium bars on the boot-top. A wrap-round chassis in black cradles the body and the wheel is simply sprung with damper and rocking pivot. Watsonian-Squire used to make the RS3 which had a child's dicky seat at the rear.

The RX4 is much larger, although not a virtual one-wheeled people-carrier like the Oxford DL. It was developed about 15 years ago in conjunction with EZS in Holland, at a time when Watsonian-Squire also imported the EZS Sovereign. Its 30 inch wide seat can take an adult and small child and, like the Sovereign, it has a vast, high boot and stream-lined, modern mudguard. Unlike the Sovereign, which had lights faired into the sidecar nose, the RX4 carries its winkers and side and stop lights within the mudguard, like the ST3. It has hidden hinges which enable a lot of the scuttle to open

Left, an RX4 on the ubiquitous DragStar, and right, the neat Squire ST3 on a Suzuki sports tourer.

Top left, Piaggio scooter with Squire PV1 micro-chair (attached to the bike by a single hefty tube), the inheritor of the early 1960s Watsonian Bambini. Top right, the Watsonian Monza sporting the classic 1950s design of mudguard (originally pressed steel but now fibre-glass) and 10 inch steel wheel with period chrome trim disc - Watsonian-Squire's best-value and most attractive chair in my opinion, here on a Harley Dyna. Bottom left, the GP Sports classic single seater: the grab handle, alloy step, Union Jack and flared mudguard are all extra Jubilee fittings. (Photos courtesy of Watsonian-Squire)

with the screen. These are terrific chairs - popular with dyed-in-the-wool sidecarrists, and are seen partnered with many modern bikes, especially Metric and Harley cruisers. They really suit modern designs, but look a little bizarre with older classic machines which they tend to overwhelm - like a tall, busty starlet with her ancient, wrinkled husband.

The Squire PV1 is for those who wish to fit a chair to a scooter - it is a microscopic blob of a sidecar, which rather illustrates my feeling that outfits need to be a certain size. The scooter/micro-chair combo has never seemed to have much appeal aesthetically or mechanically - a fact as true in the late '50s when the Swallow Sprite was available as it is today, judging by sales. It's partly because the very low power of such an outfit makes it restricted in its field of operation. 'Put-putting' through the cobbled back streets of Florence it might make sense; on London's M25 freeway it doesn't. The '60s way of attaching a chair - using a single rigid steel tube with hefty fittings - always looked rather temporary and flimsy, although it probably wasn't. Scooters present problems because of that bodywork, but the new breed of super-scooters with motors of 500cc, such as the Yamaha T-Max or Suzuki Burgman can be seen both triked and attached to sidecars.

The bulk of Watsonian-Squire's remaining output is firmly targeted at the big retro/cruiser segment and nearly all their chairs look pretty good with nearly all the bikes to which they are commonly fitted.

The old Monza design is particularly attractive and is at home on modern Triumph Thunderbirds and Bonnevilles, on Japanese cruisers or on genuine '60s iron. The Monza is an excellent chair, best in its first early '60s configuration (still available) with 10 inch steel wheel, chromed hub-cap and fibre-glass copy of the original pressed-steel streamlined mudguard. The wrap-round Silk chassis looks really nice with a chromed front perimeter and the general finish is of high quality. Carpet, soft seating and a chromed grab-rail are all attractive features. The one I owned in the late '90s had only one fault: a poorly-sewn hood which left a leak-prone hole at the near-side plastic window - a fact I became aware of only once, after the guarantee period had elapsed, when it rained. The Monza weighs about 14 stone, which makes it suitable for most bikes of 650cc upwards, although I must say that I found that 1000cc was more realistic for a chair of this weight and track. In plain black it is as stylish as anything on the street and, with a genuine classic Norton, Panther or BSA Golden Flash, it is as effective a head-turner as you could wish.

The format is continued in another of Watsonian's offerings, the GP Sports with octagonal nose. This sidecar apes the 'zeppelin' style of the German Steib 350/501 and the Garrard of the 1950s and to many older peoples' eyes is the definitive shape of the 'real' sidecar. Originally offered with 10 inch wheel and streamlined spat, it has recently (since 1992 or thereabouts) been available with a spoked 16 inch wheel and slimmer mudguard. In this form it is known as the GP Jubilee. This makes for a much nicer set-up, in my eyes. The classic 1930s zeppelin shape needs spokes and a large side-wheel to set it off. I possessed a very jolly one hitched to an Indian Enfield 500 at the beginning of the '90s. I recall Peter Rivers-Fletcher's comment (he was MD of Watsonian-Squire at that time): "This is the sort of work we like doing: creating simple classic outfits as in the good old days." He probably said that sort of thing to all his customers, but it's true that the Royal Enfield Bullet 500/GP Jubilee combo is a very successful time-warp indeed - 'a living dinosaur', as one journalist put it. It's still available, because Watsonian are the UK's Royal Enfield importers, and is best with the Electra version of the bike.

The wide-bodied *GP 700* suits bigger machines. When you look, you see them everywhere that sidecars gather. They are on Bandits, on Harleys, on VN 1500s, on Goldwings, on Triumph Legends - some riders even pair them with smaller machines, such as the Kawasaki W650; I had one on a DragStar 650 (the very one which had nearly done 48 counties in 48 hours hitched to a Matchless, in emulation of a similar feat decades before, and reported in *The Classic Motorcycle*), but I thought the bike lacked the capacity to provide the requisite 'oomph' for it. I've also tried this sidecar

Top left, the Monaco, with lifting screen and scuttle. Top right, the Palma with child's seat in place of the Monaco's boot, with alternative wheel choices clearly visible. Bottom left the Manx showing its abbreviated tail and on the right, the little Stratford on a Yamaha 535 Virago cruiser. (Photos of Monaco, Palma and Stratford courtesy of Watsonian-Squire)

on a 500cc single, but that wasn't a success either. Its track is too wide and it seems (although it isn't) appreciably heavier than its narrower sibling. This is, I reckon, because the effective weight of bell-crank, damper, wheel, mudguard and associated metalwork is further out. The chair comes near to dwarfing a middle-size bike. As I've mentioned already, Watsonian-Squire sold it in 2006 coupled to a Yamaha XVS1100 as a complete unit, so that's the sort of size of bike with which it should be used.

The other old '60s designs still in production are the single-seat Monaco and the twin-seat Palma. For each there is a choice of wheel and mudguard. The Monaco has the same dimension as the Monza, but has two features the Monza doesn't. Its windscreen and scuttle lift to help entry and exit (although the release of the catches really needs someone to help from outside) and it has a usefully large boot. The Monza's luggage compartment is reached in the old-fashioned way, by tipping forward the seat squab: cheap, effective, weather-proof, but annoying for a passenger if the pilot suddenly wants the folding hood or a spanner. The GP models have small, sloping boots with exterior lockable panel (a feature which adds a surprising amount to the purchase price). The Monaco has a lockable lid and deep, square storage area. If you buy one, you should order it with the period small wheel and replica mudguard. It looks odd and high-perched with the 16 inch spoked wheel that suits the GP.

The Palma is substantially the same as the Monaco, but with a child's seat where the boot would be. This sidecar has no tonneau, but a canvas-duck roof which most people keep in place. It's jolly low though, unless your passenger is tiny. Some complain about scuttle shake when in motion, others think the raised screen doesn't make exit all that easy; and when you're in either of these models you feel cut off by the large wrap-round Perspex area. Many passengers prefer the 'fairground ride' openness and sense of speed given by the shorter, flatter screens of the Monza and GP Sports. In recent years Watsonian-Squire have offered a DL version of the Palma and Monaco which features a lower, flatter nose in place of the bulbous 'dolphin' snout of the original.

These models are at the centre of this manufacturer's range and are each attractive in their different ways. Having owned several of them I would, however, plump for the Monza. It suits both medium and big bikes, neither dwarfed, nor dwarfing. It's cheaper, simpler, more fun to ride in and arguably more stylish than the others. Certainly it's the one I've enjoyed most. I bought my first one second-hand in 1973 and last one new in 2000.

The final choices you have are newcomers to the Watsonian range: the GP Manx and the Stratford. These answer what the manufacturers must feel is a call for smaller, lighter chairs. The Manx is a short-tailed version of the GP featuring a very stubby rear with boot reached via the seat squab. I've seen a few of these around, but I've yet to be convinced that the shortened shape is very attractive. Funnily enough, nearly all the ones I've had a chance to examine have been on quite big bikes: Moto Guzzi 850s and Harleys, for example.

The Stratford is a very neat small chair, but has the air of being built down to a price, which the Manx doesn't. Its mudguard bolted straight on to the side, its little fender attached to the body by three metal prongs, its rubber suspension - all these smack of economy/utility but without style. However I've also seen a fair number of these where sidecar riders gather, so it must sell. And it had a recent good review in a classic motorcycle magazine hitched to the, then new, Rotax-powered MZ single.

That pretty well completes what models you could get now new, or very recent second-hand, from the old pioneering firm of Watsonian-Squire. They are very pleasant to deal with, work quickly and will make every effort to put together what you require. Perhaps because of their long history of making sidecars, Watsonian-Squire favour the old fashioned method of attaching the sidecar to the bike using clamps for many of their sidecars.

UNIT Sidecars

This brings me to the next major manufacturer of sidecars in Britain: Unit Sidecars of Sible Hedingham, Essex. They have made their name over the last twenty or more years by, among other innovations, offering an absolutely simple and fool-proof method of attachment and removal of their chairs from bikes. They don't use clamps, swan-necks or odds and ends of shifting tubes. When you take your bike to them, assuming it has a fairly conventional frame, they weld triangular struts at 90 degrees to the ground at four points on the bike. The sidecar has non-adjustable bottom legs with U-bolts that mate directly onto the lower pair of these struts, and adjustable rods, the U-bolts of which can be screwed in and out, which mate directly onto the upper pair of struts. Four short bolts with neoprene lock-nuts secure each U-bolt, and that's it. Because the struts are the same angle and the U-bolts can rotate relative to them, they all come off together and all go back together. Sidecar and bike remain in constant alignment however often you separate them and the operation can be done by one person. If you pull all four bolts out, unplug the electrical feed and let the chair's chassis-rail drop onto thick cushion pads, you can just lean the bike away from the chair and wheel it away. Re-attachment involves wheeling the bike back to a spot where the lower U-bolts slide back into position. You pop their bolts in, and then manoeuvre the bike struts into the top U-bolts.

Unit produce four models, and, as I have mentioned with regard to Watsonian-Squire's Monza, I find that their nicest chair is not necessarily their most expensive. I guess that it's quite hard to make a capacious-booted, high-roofed sidecar a thing of felicitous parts.

Recently Unit have partnered a Triumph Rocket III with a chair which involved making an even fatter, higher and heavier version of their Hedingham XL. The resultant combo was fairly spectacular. I saw it at London's Ace Café Sidecar Day in 2006 and was quite impressed, although, to be honest, I thought the bike would have looked just as nice with a slimmer, sleeker chair. The problem with the Rocket III, as with so many large-capacity modern machines, is that, while they make ideal sidecar tugs, they either have virtually no visible frame on which to attach the chair, or their vast engines bulge out so much that attachment is tricky. As with Panther 100s and 120s from the late '50s and early '60s, it is generally possible to use the engine itself as a stressed member and bolt one or more of the sidecar attachments directly to it. UNIT is now putting this large version of the Hedingham XL into limited production for Rocket fanciers.

The core of the UNIT range is the versions of the attractive sports chair. The Hedingham SS, first designed by Keith Wash in 1974, features perimeter tubing, rather like most of Watsonian's models, but instead of using a swing-arm and sprung damper for suspension, a steel torsion-bar is incorporated into the rear members of the frame and the wheel attached to that. The result is great rigidity and long, maintenance-free

Left. Unit Sidecars Hedingham SS on a handsome Moto Guzzi, with Unit forks . Right the Hedingham XL, a very purposeful single seat tourer. Note the wealth of safety tubing, the sturdy aluminium step, the cavernous boot, the high roof-line and the forward tilting scuttle and screen, for easy access, and Unit forks again. Note too the chair mounted spotlights on these two outfits, and although you cannot see it here, both outfits are colour matched.

life. The frontal area of the sidecar body or boat is reminiscent of those racing cars of the mid-20th century - low and long. The wheels can be either spoked or aluminium slotted-disc and there are fitment points for additional spotlights. All Hedinghams have capacious boots, but the Hedingham XL's is especially huge. The absence of conventional springing and associated castings means that the chairs are lighter than similar sized ones from other makes and they manage to look good on both new and classic motorcycles. These chairs can be - and usually are - fitted with wheel brakes. They feature UNIT's simple, straight-arm U-bolt fittings and are easy to disassemble and refit. A purist who loves clean lines might feel that there is rather too much welded-on bent tubing around the perimeter of these chairs, but these act both as useful grab-holds and as safety buffers.

New for 2009 is the XL Mk II. This has a fixed roof and screen which, with the scuttle, tip back to enable easy access. Hydraulic struts support the weight and the passenger can open up from within - a rare feature. There's a choice of chassis for this one: the standard perimeter frame with torsion-bar springing or a box-frame with a shock absorber and trailing arm.

UNIT also manufacture a tall sidecar, the ETH, designed for attachment to BMW boxers and derived from off-road and grass-track racing. Actually, although they are an absolute contrast from UNIT's very low standard models, they are fun to ride in, and it's nice for the passenger to be on the same level as the pilot for a change. They are basic, however, with nothing in the way of weather protection. Someone who likes sidecars commented to me that the front of the ETH looks like a 1950s fridge on the move.

Top, Unit's ETH attached to a BMW 1150 Boxer, for which it was designed. This chair is thought by some to be an ungainly beast, but I rather like the seat height. The whole thing has a slight flavour of those 'sociable chairs' of 1910. Below is the runt of Unit's litter: the charming (and inexpensive) Sprite, the lines of which complement both classic and retro-styled cruisers very well indeed. This model has a box chassis and exposed leading link suspension, not a torsion bar as on the rest of Unit's sports range.

UNIT's final offering is my favourite from their range, the Sprite. This was conceived as a light chair suitable for 500cc or 650cc classic machines. Its design owes something to Charnwood's Meteor, for it has the same striking, streamlined pointed tail - reminding one of those Brookland's racers of the 1920's - and owes something to classic Indian motorbikes, for it has a very Indian-esque mudguard; but the front is pure Hedingham, with a very low, racing-car nose. Unlike the standard SS and XL range, the Sprite has been given a different chassis in square-section framing. I recall the designer of Kenna sidecars in the USA (now being manufactured again by Dauntless Motors) pointing out that square-sectioning is very suitable for sidecar construction. It is rigid and doesn't need to cope with the sort of bend-stresses which round tubing can do on bike frames. The Sprite chassis has conventional damper and rocking-arm suspension with a 16 inch un-braked, spoked wheel. Although designed for medium bikes, it looks particularly attractive on larger ones too - especially cruisers, the 'retro' lines of which it suits.

Unlike the cheaper offerings from Watsonian-Squire, UNIT do not finish off the Sprite with interior carpet. Just a seat and squab is provided, so you have to sort out your own floor-covering if you want it. It is even lighter than the SS - barely 9 stone - so the bike is hardly aware of it. It detaches in less than 10 minutes. The chair is too small to be very useful for touring purposes and it doesn't have a hood, just a tonneau, so really it comes squarely into that category of sidecar which is fitted largely for the enjoyment of the rider, but since I've had one, it has had more flattering comments than any chair I've owned, cheap runt of the litter though it may be. It is being redesigned for 2009 with a slightly higher seat.

If UNIT products have one Achilles-heel, it is their method of windscreen attachment. Watsonian have aluminium-framed perspex windscreens which are attached directly to the dash of the body. They are handsome and rigid. UNIT bend their flexible plastic screen round the *outside* of the raised dash and attach it with plastic screws. After a time, dust, leaves, insects and road dirt find their way between the screen and the body-work. The effect is grubby. You can undo the screen and clean up, but it's a chore and those plastic bolts don't look that durable. A useful tip is to press, with a screwdriver, a strand of plastic-covered wire, preferably of the chair's colour, between screen and dashboard. This seals that dust trap for quite a long time. A further annoying feature is that UNIT's screen is bendy and one has to discourage passengers from using it as a support when clambering in and out.

UNIT build to order and fit over a 10 day period. You may have to wait 12 weeks from first order to collection. This is likely with all the sidecar makers in Britain. In general, their establishments are on the lines of a cottage industry employing a small number of people. The positive side of this is that the individuals concerned with design, welding and assembly are experienced enthusiasts, and the customer's requirements are never too much trouble. It is, however, pointless to expect a take-away speed service; their order books are often full and some of their commissions demand a lot of ingenuity and time.

UK imports.

There are some fairly common makes of continental sidecars available in Britain, and this provision is what the other sidecar dealerships specialise in. For good commercial reasons the biggest Swiss, German and Dutch firms don't have much impact in the UK, but the erstwhile Eastern bloc makers, like Velorex and Ural do. These have their virtues.

As has been previously mentioned, it is against the law to fit a right hand sidecar in the UK which can rather limit the UK market for some of the sidecars available in Europe and the USA, for example. Imports seem to occupy positions at the furthest poles of their markets: cheap 'n' cheerful (£1,500) or super-de-luxe (£10,000).

Chang Jiang

These Chinese machines are very similar to the Ural in that both are copies of early BMW and Steib military sidecars. They are relatively cheap and imported through BEMW, Derby and MPC of Leicester.

EML

EML sidecars and trikes are made in Holland and used to be imported by EW Pinchbeck. EML now make some left hand sidecars for sale in the UK, and trike conversions for the Goldwing imported by Colin Appleyard of Keighley in West Yorkshire.

A beautiful double seater EML attached to a Kawasaki 1100cc sports tourer, complete with seat-belts for fast, safe motoring. The Dutch make some of the world's best chairs and, currently, the products of both EML and EZS are available for left-hand use in the UK.

EZS

Again made in Holland, this company makes some impressive sidecars which are sold in the UK through Watsonian-Squire and Charnwood. EZS' Munro sidecar is supplied fitted to a Triumph Rocket III by Watsonian to create a luxury combination, and Charnwood have a range of bikes to which they can fit the EZS Munro.

EZS Munro and Triumph 2300cc Rocket III as supplied by Watsonian-Squire in the UK at a cost of £22,000 or so at 2007 prices. Costly perfection.

Ural

My favourite of the imported chairs is that Russian Ural I have referred to earlier, a copy of Steib's military sidecar as fitted to WWII BMW and Zundapp boxers. All current sidecars make use of fibre-glass for their bodywork - not surprisingly, in view of the ease with which any shape can be created. The Ural chair is different. It is solid steel and monstrously heavy. There may be something in that old urban myth that the factories of the USSR reached their manufacturing quotas through the amount of raw materials they consumed, rather than units produced, and that you couldn't saw through a Ural tube because it was virtually solid. I have found it impossible to pick-up a 1972 Ural sidecar chassis frame plus wheel, and the Ural metal body alone takes two to lift.

Usually exported specifically for attachment to Ural or (now obsolete) Dnepr machines, it uses the ball and rose system for the two lower fitments, and straight struts and U-bolts for the upper ones. It can be made to fit other bikes with judicious use of clamps. The importers can advise on this. These chairs have something of the grand old days of charioteering about them. They are high-set on a 19 inch spoked wheel, are very easy to step into and have a lockable boot, all-weather vinyl seat and rubber flooring and a basic pane and vinyl apron screen. Like Velorexes, they are very good value. I do recommend their use on something with a bit more guts than the Ural though (although the complete outfit looks marvellous) because of their weight. If ever there was a sidecar to see out the end of all motoring to the beginning of the next Ice Age, this is it. Ural bikes and sidecars are imported by F2 (Banbury), MPC (Leicester), and C&C (Maidstone).

Velorex

These are currently imported by F2 Motorcycles and are available in three forms: a single-seat light sports with low screen, a high-screened version of this and an even bigger model with faired-in wheel and tall back. The cheapest is the most attractive to my eyes - its low screen and large wheel are quite 'period' looking. The large closed rear tourer is striking, but not elegant. All three attach by clamps with a good variety

Top, the nicest looking Velorex, the low boot, single-seat sports, here fitted to a classic BSA single. Below, the other Velorex, here on a 350cc two-stroke Jawa for which it was designed. Although you do see Velorex chairs on big cruisers, they were intended for low-powered bikes, as their slim fittings suggest

of fitments available. They are good value, but they need to be kept clean and attention must be given fairly often to clamp tightness. They were originally designed for haulage by Czech Jawa 350cc two-strokes, so they are not framed for high-speed cornering with heavy loads and high-capacity machines, although the last one I saw was fitted perfectly securely to a Harley-Davidson 'Electraglide' and looked quite at home.

UK second hand market

So far, I've concentrated on new products currently available from stock or to order, but, just as in the far past, the last 20 years of British motorcycling have had their ephemeral sidecar makers come and go. Most of the major companies who were, until recently, in business are listed here. There are of course literally scores of others.

Briggs

The pumped-on-steroids heavyweight of late designs was the Briggs Dolphin, a copy, like the contemporary Yates saloon, of the 1961 Canterbury 'Carmobile'. Briggs Sidecars also made a little Swift chair, but it was not a good-looker. The large Dolphin was better, but lacked the genuine urbanity of the huge 3-4 seater Carmobile - guaranteed to dwarf completely any contemporary family car parked next to it, let alone the bike to which it was attached. Both Yates and Briggs did their best to emulate the road-presence of the really big sidecar from the days before the BMC Mini. Like a genuine Canterbury, their saloons were made of light metal over a wooden frame with car-type wheel set into the body. With their 'suicide' front doors and an interior larger than a Ford Escort van, they really were as near to classic as you could get bolted to a motorcycle.

Martello Sidecars

Made by Martello Plastics in Folkstone, Kent, their single-seat saloon had a short vogue in the 1980s and resembled a halved Reliant 'Robin' without the front wheel. It was rather fun, completely waterproof and nicely built, with its car-type 10 inch

A Martello sidecar attached to a BMW. Once the passenger has been battened down in this plastic spaceship, he or she is in a separate world

wheel set within the bodywork and single nose-mounted headlight. It looked pretty good with biggish modern bikes, although it was best without the optional child seat extension, the square lines of which spoilt the rakish high-set moulded body-line. Their sidecar is still listed on their website as a bespoke product, but it has been a long time since I have seen one.

Side-Rider

The Side-Rider had an extremely late '70s/early '80s 'Matchbox Toys Speed-Wheels' look, and its totally enclosed narrow-windowed 'pod' must have been best for those with extreme agoraphobia. It featured monocoque construction again, with wheel under the upward-sweeping body-side - that *leitmotif* of '80s sidecar design.

Wasp Sidecars

Made by R. Rhind-Tutt of Wasp Motorcycles, Salisbury, Wiltshire, Wasp sidecars were designed for off-road sidecar trials work, but their road-going sports single-seater was very pretty and went well with modern bikes. I've seen several, but they've always

The elegant Wasp single-seater made by R Rhind-Tutt in Wiltshire, an organisation better known for its competition sidecars, attached here to a Kawasaki sports tourer via a specially manufactured frame. It isn't easy fitting a chair to a bike with total bodywork enclosure - although ways are always found.

been black, irrespective of the bike's colour (unless, of course, I've been seeing the same one on a succession of different machines; there isn't a way of telling). Wasp still make competition trials outfits (see *Sidecar and Trike Contacts*)

Wessex Sidecars

P J Turner Motorcycles of Lyme Regis, Dorset, brought back a famous name. The original Wessex was one of the late '50s most admired chairs with a passing resemblance to the Daimler Dart sports car of the era. It had an attractive streamlined mudguard, ample cock-pit glass and a well-made cast step. What made it really different was that it had no perimeter chassis; seven short struts attached directly to its body - an attribute of stressed-skin aircraft design, as motorcycle reviewers were fond of pointing out. It was considered the most rigid of all bike / chair fixing methods, although I thought it looked a pain to take on and off. The 'new' Wessex of the early 1990s followed this practice, though I find its lines less pleasing than those of the original. It could look striking when colour-matched and was certainly rakish with its alloy wheel set into the body and the 'bubble' Perspex canopy resembling the sharp end of a fighter jet.

Left, an outstanding, original late 1950s Wessex sidecar on a BMW boxer. Note the Daimler Dart like mudguard, cast step, 19 inch spoked wheel and elegant hinged glass-house. The front bumper is a later edition. These chairs were attached by no fewer than seven struts to their bike for maximum rigidity. On the right is the modern Wessex of the 1990s, here attached to one of the last resurrections of the Norton. Although striking and aerodynamic, the passenger accomodation is more claustrophobic than the cockpit of a jet fighter - which it resembles.

Where are they now?

These recent flowerings of the often ephemeral, yet strangely persistent sidecar trade, can still be found advertised in the back pages of *Old Bike Mart*, *Classic Bike Guide* or *RealClassic Magazine* and many others. Firms like Charnwood Classic Restorations are often able to find one for you - or, if you're lucky - have one in stock second-hand. A list of suitable magazines is given at the back of the book (see pages 129-133)

Jeff Clew in *Motorcycling in the Fifties* asked, in a chapter heading, the question: 'Whatever happened to the sidecar?' In the late 1950s and early '60s there were a dozen manufacturers and nearly 200,000 combinations on British roads. Many of these must have dated from the '40s when a third of all motorcycles had a sidecar fitted to them. By 1970 they'd all gone. Part of the answer to Jeff Clew's question is: they fell apart and rotted away. The quality of construction of some of the so-called 'coach built' chairs was of very questionable quality. They had cheap butt joints, frames of unseasoned wood, flimsy rust-prone steel panels, primitive Cobex screens which cracked in the sun and canvas roofs which rotted in the rain. Those which had suspension used wobbly Gregoire-link systems (introduced as late as 1954 by Canterbury, because before that time the wheel was mounted on a stub axle which shook the frame to bits). Flaking cart-springs kept chassis and body apart while seized bolts, bald tyres, ripped seats and cracked tubes completed the pretty typical down-market sidecar. Who was going to preserve and restore such hen-coops in the glowing era of the Ford Cortina and Vauxhall Victor?

Some of the period's new-fangled fibre-glass confections, pioneered by Swallow and Watsonian, did survive - and you can still see a few. Their finish may be a little crazed and their chassis may not be creak-free, but they've made it into the 21st century. Yet to what end? Every attractive design of the 'good old days' is now replicated with better materials, and people buy their sidecar to set off their immaculate cruiser or tourer. Your GoldWing is not improved by bolting on a sagging, faded, forty-year old relic. Sometimes, an intrepid connoisseur will build his or her own, and like self-welded trikes, the end result can be fairly horrendous. This need not always be so, especially if old plans and a modern chassis are used, but, for all practical purposes - and because we're all so comparatively rich now - we might as well buy new or nearly-new.

European Manufacturers

Armec

Naturally Armec, which has an excellent website, is well to the fore. Some of their most popular models are the Tremola II and III, big luxurious carpeted chairs with side-by-side seating, massive trunk, reading lights, sunroof and carefully calibrated suspension. Armecs feature racing-car-like noses with lights set into a crash-absorbing fitting. They mount rigidly onto the bike and ride on wide-tyred alloy wheels. Armec America will harness them to most big machines, but their most stunning package is the Boss Hoss/Tremola II combination to which I have already referred. New for 2008 is the 4-seater 'Stradale' with crumple-zone, progressive suspension and hydraulic brake. The 'Sidewinder', which enables its bike to lean, is currently only available for boxer BMWs and Moto Guzzis.

Just to make the point that you see more sidecar outfits in some continental countries than in Britain, here's a family on their BMW/Steib passing a parked Moto Guzzi/Armec combo near Spiez, Switzerland. Note the gap between the bike and Armec to take account of the lean of the machine over the sidecar, because this is one of those set ups which keeps the chair level while the rider tilts.

EML

EML sidecars are manufactured in Neede, Holland. They produce the Speed 2000 range of sidecars which are basically a single seat open sidecar with canvas type roof in a number of widths and sizes. The larger chairs feature ventilation and heating. The Dutch are still great sidecar enthusiasts, doubtless assisted by their flat country, and their equipment is of the highest quality. They also offer the E2000 for off road work.

EZS

EZS is another Dutch company and have a range of sidecars from the Compact – a small, economy model to the more luxuriously appointed Sovereign, Summit and Munro. The Munro is a twin seat open sidecar imported into the UK and can be fitted either on the left or right. It has an ingenious optional extra fuel tank which fits into the unused wheel arch. The Sovereign is a substantial sidecar which can seat a child and adult and is left hand fitting only, whilst the Summit is again a large family chair and has the distinguishing feature that the entire front of the chair lifts up for easy access. It is, though intended for right hand fitting only.

Flexit

A Dutch sidecar which leans with the bike.

Mobec

Mobec of Germany, made up a complete bike/chassis featuring the Duo-Drive transmission and Easy-Drive steering system.

A rare sight in Britain: the Flexit leaning sidecar in left-hand guise, once imported and marketed by Watsonian-Squire, here mounted on a Honda Pan-European. This shot shows well the uncanny impression this chair gives of being suspended in mid air.

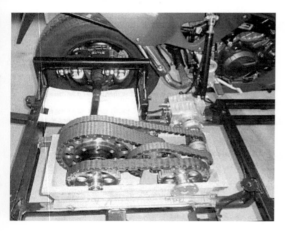

Mobec's Super-Drive box with its many forward and reverse gears (Photo courtesy of HSOC). The imput from the selection feeds the under-floor box and the drive is then split between bike rear wheel and the chair wheel. The output for this is in the foreground. This photograph illustrates the lengths to which those who wish to create outfits without compromise (and who have the requisite deep pockets) are prepared to go.

A DKW scooter made in the German Federal Republic with an ultra-light, but undeniably stylish, Steib chair from 1965.

Ideal-Motorrader & Seitenwagen (Steib)

Based in Berlin the company started manufacturing reproductions of the Steib LS200, S350, S500 and TR500 for both right and left hand mounting. The manufacturing plant is based in Poland. Euro prices for these, at the time of writing, do not seem exorbitant.

URAL

Russian made sidecars of serious weight. These have already been described in the UK Imports section above.

US Manufacturers

America is a diverse market with importers of all the major British and European makes, and quite a few interesting manufacturers of its own. It is worth noting that although it is not legal to drive a sidecar outfit in the UK with the chair on the 'wrong' side, in practice few police patrols are going to notice or care. It might, however, be rather a gamble to bring a US made chair into the UK and find you can't use it, but I've been tempted. You can see from the companies listed below, that sidecar manufacturing is still alive and well on the other side of the Atlantic. However In America, the trike is by far the more popular of the two forms of three-wheeling, and firms such as Lehman have quite extensive factories while the sidecar makers are, as in the UK, basically cottage industries.

California Sidecars

This company produce the Friendship II, Friendship III and Companion GT. They feature trailing-arm suspension and a four-point, quick-disconnect system. You can get electric lean-adjustment, disc brakes and onboard CD hi-fi player. Although rather stubby-looking from certain angles, the general effect of the broad nose rising to a high screen at the same angle is quite impressive, especially partnered with a big bike. The seat is like one of those rich, plush armchairs favoured by multi-national company tycoons.

Champion Sidecars

The 'Escort' from Champion Sidecars is about as stubby as the California Sidecars offerings and in fact very similar in looks . It too has a super seat, orthopaedically designed, and another quick-disconnect system. Champion will equip their chair to remarkably luxurious standards if you wish. This sidecar needs to partner a very big machine and, unsurprisingly, Champion make fitments for the latest Goldwing.

Left, the Dauntless Liberator with steering chair-wheel. The linkage is effected between front forks and sidecar wheel. This seems a great idea, but I've never had experience of one, so don't know how well it works (photo courtesy of Dauntless Motors). Right, the Harley Davidson R/H fitting sidecar was made in such vast numbers that it is easy enough to find one second-hand, often well restored, as this beautifully preserved outfit in Interlaken, Switzerland testifies. Fifty year old Harley combos speak volumes for the massive construction and quality of these American machines, and, Harley being Harley, they still look modern.

Creative Metal Products

Chopper style combos using intricate fabricated frames and low-slung mechanics are a feature of Creative Metal Products designs. These have no passenger accommodation and are the perfect expression of the charioteer whose mount is for himself alone.

Dauntless Motor Corp

Dauntless Motors are making the old Kenna sidecar once more, but the jewel in their crown is the Liberator. This car-like two-seater (again strangely reminiscent to British eyes of a halved Reliant Robin) has a targa top (a cabriolet version) and nice wide alloy wheel, but its real ace-in-the-hole is that this wheel is *steered* by fitment to the bike's front forks. The difference this makes to cornering can be imagined. It's a brilliant idea and I'm amazed that it hasn't caught on. Dauntless seem to be the only people to offer it at the time of writing. Unless the sidecar as a mode of transport achieves greater popularity than its current niche status, manufacturers are unlikely to invest much in unorthodox designs, however.

Hannigan Motorsports

The Hannigan, one of my favourites, is very arresting indeed with its big custom bright-alloy wheel, huge tyre, wing-like spoiler and deep nose scoops. It looks as if, instead of a carpet and footrest, it ought to have a V8 motor in its nose. The boat, or body, is a light affair on a very heavy frame with quick disconnect hardware. Standard on the touring chairs is Electronic Camber Control. Married to a modern sports-tourer its effect is easily as spectacular as a Merlin's. Startlingly different is the Hannigan TriCar, a combination of trike and sidecar with a combo's bodywork and a tricycle's equilateral wheelbase. This new device for 2008 might just catch on, but at a price.

Motorvation Engineering

Motorvation make some striking chairs - Roadster and Formula II - the sort that look fast when stationary. Their Formula II can hold an extra 10 gallon fuel system and has a flip-up nose for access. The idea of the extra fuel is very appealing, giving ballast when riding alone, and extending the range, but has not been a feature of sidecar design since Brough's fuel-in-chassis chair of the late-1930s - which just shows that there's nothing new.

SCF Sidecars

This company make a coach-built sidecar on a heavy steel frame with a body in 18-gauge steel sheet. It rides on a rubber block and torsion-bar suspension with car tyres and features touches such as polished, real wood armrests. It's exceptionally striking.

Texas Sidecar Co

The Texas Sidecar Co make the Ranger, a small, single-seat sports model not dissimilar in appearance to the UNIT Sprite, but more fully fitted-out. Its effect with a cruiser is much the same, however, although the mudguard is much less arresting, consisting merely of a blade.

Summary

In Europe, at present, sidecars are more numerous than trikes whilst in the USA trikes outnumber sidecars. In both cases, however, it has to be admitted that what interest there is in either is pretty minimal - somewhere between hang-gliding and being a Druid. One's reaction to this is either to think: 'Good, let's keep the whole thing pleasantly arcane, head-turning and exclusive', or: 'Bad, let's try to bring word of what fun three-wheeling can be to other motorcyclists'. I find I have oscillated between the two extremes, but now feel a greater urge to proselytise - hence these pages.

But that seems to have passed. Now, well into the 21st century, I like to think that the sidecar outfit is just seen as characterful - just another expression of that 'customising' of lifestyle which - according to some experts - is going to be as important a segmentising or 'signposting' of the individual in society, as Henry Ford's contribution towards homogenisation and standardisation was nearly 100 years ago.

Two views of what, in the event turned out to be blind alleys. Top, that rare survivor a 1930s Brough 750cc water-cooled four with its twin rear wheels, hitched to a period Watsonian chair - altogether more impressive and desirable than the spindly Austin Seven from which the motor came. The bike, it was said, could be driven as a solo - it was, after all a sort of trike - but cornering involved tipping it up onto one of its closely spaced back wheels.

Below, the wide tracked and capable 1942 military Zundapp and powered sidecar. Note the two gear selectors on the tank and interchangeable spare tyre. Many believed these flexible, torquey 750cc boxers had the edge on the cheaper Jeep over rough ground.

WHAT AND HOW MUCH SHALL I MODIFY?

Trikes

Nothing that comes next assumes that you are making a trike from scratch in your garden shed or garage. Such is the level of equipment and expertise required to do this effectively, let alone attractively, that it would take a great deal more space than the page or two I propose to expend here on trike modification.

No, what I mean by this section is: how much you will instruct your trike builder to incorporate into your commission from him and how much you will subsequently feel like doing when you get the trike home and have used it for a while. My other assumption is that we are discussing bike-conversion trikes, not car-based ones.

Starting from the front

Your bike's stock front end may require one of several modifications to make your machine sweet-steering and easy to park and manoeuvre. If you have a large diameter spoked wheel - say 21 inch, as on a Harley-Davidson Night Train, you will need to consider the lateral stresses on those spokes. A stubbier wheel with short spokes will be tough enough, but a change to a machined alloy wheel may have to come high on your list. If you wish to retain a large spoked wheel, you will need a new rim laced much more densely than normal for solo use. Check out Compomotive wheels or try AMS Precision for what's in stock.

You may not have to change your mudguard, but if you do, make sure that it will stop road dirt and water spraying up over the motor. Luckily, there is a vogue for retro-styled sweeping tin-ware at present. It does a much better job than a skimpy, quarter-circumference blade.

You might need to change the stock bike's brakes if you have changed the wheel. This might be the moment to specify an upgrade to high-performance 4 and 6 piston calipers such as French-made Beringers, available from Zodiac in polished black or

A hefty Reliant conversion. Notice the very upright posture of the forks compared with those on the Triumph parked nearby. Practically zero trail such as this would make for light steering, but those long tiller-bars would be necessary to keep the plot running in a stright line - the castor action of the wheels would be pretty strong. Note too the massive exposed fork springs to cope with the weight of frame and motor

chrome. Harrison Billet 6, cut from solid metal are widely known. Many owners take the opportunity to replace rubber brake hoses with metal ones from firms like Venhill.

The weight of a trike is not borne by the front end, so it may not be necessary to change your stock machine's fork springs, however some trike firms will fit leading-link forks if you ask them to, on the grounds that the steering will be less heavy. Be warned, however, that leading-links and a pretty front end seldom go together. It may be better to change the stock handle-bars to wider ones for leverage, and to raise them and bring them nearer to you. PhatRisers from Scootworks in the USA, do just that and are very well made. To firm up the twin legs of a telescopic fork, try a support bar just above the mudguard, like the Super Brace, also available from America.

It has been my experience that deciding on a steeply-raked fork is counter-productive. The expense and extra metal-work needed to strengthen the original head-stock is one thing, but the lack of nimbleness on the trike is another. A steep fork will just make parking and going round corners awkward and annoying. It looks great on show trikes, and seems to lend itself to US ideas of cruising, but in reality the trail and rake of the stock machine will prove to be the best.

The engine and ancillaries

One of the first things that a customiser thinks of doing to his newly-emerging mount is to make it both louder and more powerful. I can see why the whisper-quiet rustlings of all Euro 3 compliant modern bikes seems to go against the spirit of 'notice-me' which customising is all about, although it's never struck me as logical that while the muscular silence of a Rolls Royce is admired, the same thing in a bike isn't. As for making the engine more powerful, is it not more reasonable to buy a more powerful beast in the first place, rather than wring dynamics from a design which might prove better if not more highly-stressed? However, assuming the twin urges above are irresistible, there are ways of setting about things which won't wreck reliability and bank-balance.

Exhaust

After-market cans are often more free-flowing than stock ones, but may require the motor to be re-mapped. Avoid re-mapping or re-jetting where possible - it's seldom as straight-forward as it sounds. An upping of bhp is less necessary for three-wheeled use than torque and may prove that final straw too much for an engine which is going to have to work harder anyway. After-market silencers, especially for cruisers, do not necessarily require changes to carbs and timing. Jardine's retro pipes for the Honda VTX spring to mind. Doctor Dragstar offers internal surgery on the stock pipes to free up a little more urge and a little more sound, but no other changes are needed. Custom Cruisers offers push-button exhausts in which an electric valve routes the gases either straight through or round the baffles for those occasions when noise is a must.

Once you could get 55bhp at the output gear from a bellowing BSA 500cc Gold Star, now such an output is the norm from the engines of V-twin cruisers of more than 1200cc. But think back to how noisy the old Beezer was, how prone to breakdown, how inflexible in traffic, how uncontrollable at low speeds, how uncomfortable at high ones! The way forward, at the moment, seems to be with muffled, under-stressed, lean-burn cubes.

Remember, too, that the continued acceptance of biking in all its forms is largely conditional on us not annoying the majority. Our law-makers equate noise with hooliganism and danger and nothing's going to change that. More than once, as I've passed people on ultra-silent modern cruisers, I have heard them say to each other, "That's a nice, quiet bike." Such comments are the orthodoxy, whatever we think.

Intake

Before you tear off the restrictive air filters on your machine, bear in mind that unfiltered air will wreck engines in months. Some air-cleaners were so restricted as to be absurd - like the Fiat car unit stuck on the last incarnation of the Moto Guzzi Falcone - but manufacturers now have done their homework, much as after-market tuners would like you to believe the opposite. When you decide to replace your stock cleaner with some smart new kit, make sure it does the same job as the one you have removed. An expense on this sort of accessory is purely cosmetic; only by making major changes to injection is any gain in performance going to come about. It may not be all that desirable in a real-world trike to make it anything other than flexible and easy to drive.

Gear-changing

If the usual shifting up and down with the left foot leaves you tired, and you long for the ease of the sort of automatic which is common on big scooters, there is always the option of fitting an electronic shifter. The KlikTronic, made by Adaptive Motorcycling LLC of Stockholm, is a handle-bar push-button installation activating a small vertical cylinder above the gearlever. This single device handles all changes up and down more quickly than you can foot-change. It makes trike driving even more relaxing and pleasant.

Nearly all trike builders offer a reverse gear - usually an electric adaption of the final drive. It's not particularly necessary for a normal-sized bike conversion, but if you are small and the machine is heavy, it helps. Trikes based on the Ural Gear-Up motorcycle combo have it already built in, as do GoldWings.

Two unlikely, but useful add-ons

If you have been used to foot-pegs only, the pleasure of footboards will come as a revelation. Pegs dig into the arch of the foot and leave toes and heels suspended. You can't feel squarely seated with pegs. Boards are not much use with boxers, nor with trikes based on sports tourers, if the original driving position is left untouched. But if the handle-bars are widened and pulled back, as suggested for ease of steering, then the driving position will become more upright. The addition of footboards, from Highway Hawk or Zodiac or, if converting a cruiser, from your manufacturer's own accessories, will make a huge difference to comfort and confidence - especially on long distances. It is best to resist the temptation to fit foot-forward pegs in the American custom fashion - they put all your weight on the base of the spine. 'Butt-burn', as the Yanks call it, is the outcome.

The other simple add-on I would recommend is a small sheet of aluminium - which could be sprayed black - on the front frame from about the height of the front wheel axle to the bottom of the engine, under which it should curve slightly like a bash-plate. This cheap trick saves hours of cleaning after use on muddy and wet roads because it takes all the muck thrown up by the front wheel. However capacious the mudguard, there's always spray-back and it ruins exhaust down-pipes and pits the starter-motor and engine sump.

The back half of the trike

As I have pointed out already, the rear axle and its mounting will be the most important adaptation to the standard bike. If your machine is shaft-driven, the obvious next step is a limited slip differential. All the trike builders are experienced in setting these up - often of readily available Ford provenance. Some builders will use your bike's belt-drive, but others, like BB Customs and Trike Design, point out that if your belt breaks while on holiday, that's the end of it, whereas a chain can be repaired on the spot. To that end they make specially-machined sealed chain-driven differentials with hefty O-rings which require little maintenance.

The thing you need to decide on quite early is whether you want your axle mounted in line with the original one, that is: under the old wheel arch, or further back, effectively making a long-wheelbase trike. Opinions vary about this - and they are partly aesthetic and partly practical.

I think that a trike which has the same wheel-base as a bike looks pleasing and remains manoeuvrable, so I would commission a trike with its axle in the same plane as the original one. The manufacturers who do this will also be able to utilise the existing suspension and swing-arm mounting points. This may make it easier to revert, if required. It is also worth remembering that a handbrake is a legal requirement in the UK.

Taking the axle out beyond the end of the old mudguard creates a long machine which is stable at speed, but less good at nippy manoeuvres. It will also require considerable re-building, have more unsprung weight and can leave odd looking gaps unless very expertly done. As a general rule, I would only attempt a lengthened chassis if full bodywork were to be involved.

This Triumph triple has the now classic horizontal twin shock rear end. This set up, reminiscent of that used in Formula 1, really keeps the rear end down. Note the chain driven differential

Suspension and mud-guarding

The main trike makers have their own designs and those which remain in business will have thought out which make of dampers to use, and how to suspend wheels. Trike Design, for instance, model their rear ends on Formula 1 cars with suspension laid down working off the A-frame, and others have followed suit. Where your input is important is to encourage your builder to fashion practical mudguards which match the trike's front end. Wackey's Trikes design is a model of its type. There's no fun living with skimpy blades that throw up mud and water.

Loading

As a rule of thumb, trikes ride well if the sprung weight lets the suspension move over light road undulations, and the unsprung weight is kept down. I have already touched on the tax / MOT implications of weight in the UK, but what will matter in everyday use is comfort. Nothing is worse than a stiffly sprung trike with heavy axle and wheels crashing and juddering over every road ripple, especially if you mainly use it on your own. Alloy wheels help, but not if they're too wide. Twelve inch seems to be overdoing it, because the tyres will be so heavy. Seven inch looks very pleasing.

Seating is a matter of taste, but, as I have already said earlier, the original saddle, with sissy-bar for the pillion, keeps passenger weight central and the design neat. Benches not only look awkward, require lots of welded tubing to support them, and need seat-

Above, one of Wackey's Trikes' very professional conversions: Triumph's 2.3 litre Rocket III. (Photo courtesy of Wackey's)

Below, this VW-engined trike puts its carrying capacity above the motor with unmissable light-bars flanking it. This has the bonus of keeping rain off the engine and ancilliaries, but otherwise illustrates the problesm of suspension and loading. Having made this point, I would add that, provided the workmanship of all the constituent parts is of unimpeachable quality, most trikes do manage to pull off the trick of captivating the onlooker; its just that in our hypercritical visual age we have less tolerance for the Heath-Robinson style lash-up than we used to 20 or 30 years ago. That's why professional usually beats home-made.

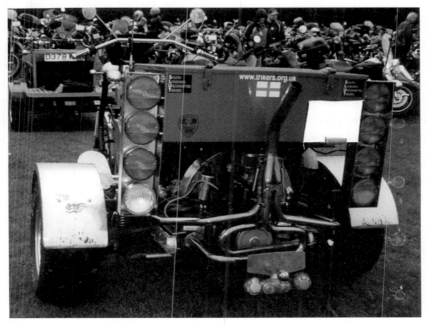

belts by law in the UK, but pose handling problems unless you transport two equally weighted individuals on each side. It's like the old joke about the roundabout and two fat men on one side of a Reliant Robin.

I can't help feeling that if you want an open-air conveyance capable of seating four, you might as well buy a convertible. A trike should remain essentially a *motorcycling* experience.

Luggage

Your choices for carrying things will be: nothing, leather saddle bags, a metal box, a trunk within encompassing bodywork. There is something rather fine and minimalist about having nothing. There's just you on your machine, with a knapsack on your shoulders if necessary. Sometimes you will want to collect shopping or go on holiday. Throw-over bags can attractively fill that space between bike rear and mudguard. A fully-booted body is luxurious and the fibre-glass will cover a multitude of welds and fitments, but you can't clean and inspect your rear end; as with a car, you can only hope it's not corroding under there. The least eye-appealing alternative is the addition of a bolted-on metal box. I've always thought that it detracts from the essential curvatures of a trike. This is an area which will need careful thrashing out with your builder.

Sidecar outfits

You will have noticed from the quick review of US sidecar manufacturers that they place a strong emphasis on quick-disconnect systems and I must admit to a liking for them myself. But this assumes that you have left your bike in stock condition and that it can instantly transform itself into a solo again.

There was a strong tradition of bolting chairs on and off in the 1920s, especially when it was still illegal to leave parked vehicles in the road overnight. The motorcycle often had several roles: a personal commuter on weekdays, a family *barouche* for trips to the sea or country on Sundays and perhaps some scrambling or track-racing on Saturday. Off and on came the chair, generally secured by one big bolt at the head-stock and two ball and rose joints lower down.

Funnily enough, it is now easier to do this in the early 21st century than it has been for decades and the reason, it seems to me, lies in recent big changes to certain types of motorcycle itself, so that your stock machine makes a very satisfactory sidecar hauler.

The AA (Automobile Association of Great Britain) for many years favoured girders and rigid rear ends, as in the photo on the left, for its huge fleet of BSA Patrol singles and box side-carriages, but eventually accepted the telescopic fork and plunger rear end (right). It was happy to keep the antique design of the BSA side-valve though.

Below, an Ariel Square Four 999cc air cooled touring machine with period Garrard single-seater. These bikes were welcomed, both before WWII when Edward Turner designed them, and after as perfect sidecar bikes. Part of the dislike of 1950s telescopics, as can be seen here, was due to their skinny flimsiness. Ariel designed some strong Earles-type leading links as an option for haulage work, but the firm ceased manufacture of the Square Four before the forks could be put into production.

Front forks: which type to specify?

In the 1950s the rigid girder-fork had given way to telescopics and the rigid rear was rapidly being replaced by sprung hubs (in the case of an experiment by Triumph), short-travel plunger (favoured by Ariel and BSA in particular) and by fully-damped swinging-arm (pioneered by Velocette and Royal Enfield). These changes were often viewed with dislike by confirmed sidecarrists who trusted the firmness of rigid bikes in corners.

The swinging-arm at the rear usually had to have its units replaced by beefier ones with harder springs, especially if the sidecar was one of those vast wallowing whales from Busmar, Blacknell or Canterbury, but it was the front fork that claimed most attention.

The 1950s and '60s front fork was often a weak, skinny affair - even those supplied for the redoubtable Panther sidecar tugs. This Dowty air-sprung fork leaked its air (not surprisingly, given the primitive material available for sealant) and the other sort, typified by the Roadholder from Norton, nearly always needed their internal springs replaced. Furthermore, these forks suffered from stiction on corners and their insubstantial triple-trees couldn't prevent 'walking', the term used to describe each fork leg trying to go its own way under the stresses and twists of uneven three-wheeled cornering.

The leading-link

Ernie Earles' leading-link fork, which had its short, load-bearing legs rigidly mounted at the end of substantial, thick blades, further supported by the mounting points of the dampers and then the wheel axle, was immune from walking, stiction and twisting. Furthermore, it was designed to give a reduced trail to the bike's front wheel. The wheel's relationship to the whole front end can be compared to the difference between those little castors at the front of a wheel chair and those on, say, a wheelbarrow. If the load 'felt' by the wheel axle is more directly above it, the wheel turns easily (as witness using a tea-trolley), but if the load is at a distance from the axle, it doesn't. (Think how annoying it can be getting a loaded wheelbarrow round a corner). Too little trail has the wheel doing what trolley wheels can do: wobble, but too much makes turning hard.

So it became a commonplace recommendation to fit Earles-type leading-links as a first adaptation of your bike to sidecar work. BMW fitted them as standard on some mid-20th century models because they assumed sidecar usage, and Ariel - too late - produced an Earles-forked Square Four model for chair work just before they went under.

For some time the leading-link fork had strong adherents in the sidecar world. The firm of UNIT *in* Essex still produces famous and very well-engineered leading-links which, they claim, make the task of steering an outfit (or trike) very much easier. Wasp Motorcycles made commonly seen forks and, as pointed out earlier, the European sidecar makers offer them too - particularly Armec, whose version is beautifully made. Ural supply outfits with their version ready-fitted.

Modern telescopics

However, for reasons not unconnected with physics, I have found that leading links just don't seem to be so necessary today. *(See the section realting to steering and trail on pages 117-118)* Any sidecar firm will both supply and fit them to order, but they don't make

This Yamaha Virago has had small lugs welded to its perimeter frame to take straight-arm fittings. Note the high mounted steering damper of the straight-through pattern. These dampers have a restricted throw, so mounting one high up between fork and bike gives increased side-to-side steering lock. A fitment up near the triple tree rather than near the bottom of the fork leg, will make flex less likely.

the difference that they did thirty or more years ago. The reasons for this are probably these: the sort of bike chosen for sidecar work is often a big, cruiser-style or touring machine - such as GoldWings, Harleys, Yamaha V-Max, Venture and DragStar, Moto Guzzi's California, Kawasaki's Drifter, Suzuki's Intruder, Triumph's Thunderbird - and what all these machines have in common (apart from the big-bore, high torque characteristics that make them good for lugging) is *very* hefty front forks. Thick walled 43mm or more diameter tubing is not uncommon. Fork legs are mounted in solid aluminium billet triple-trees. These bikes often sport substantial steel mudguards bolted to the forks halfway down, acting as reinforcement, and, of course, the fork seals and modern lubricants are miles better than they were in the '60s.

The recent fashion for near 'custom bike' angles of fork-rake has given immense amounts of straight-line stability to cruisers, so the 'fluttering' of handle-bars, once so common, has gone. In spite of the trail being as much as six inches on these machines, their steering is not anything like as heavy as you would expect. The fashion for wide US-style handlebars helps the leverage, and widespread use of a fat round front tyre on a stocky 15 inch wheel also assists. It is, perhaps, harder to steer an outfit when it is fitted with flat-section car tyres at the front. The hefty weight of modern cruiser/tourers means

Touring Armec Tremola on a Yamaha V-Max. Look at those beautifully machined gold and silver variants on leading-link forks - the simplicity of telescopics with the rigidity of the braced horizontal beams - the car wheel with flat-tread tyres, and that racing-car nose of the big double-seater chair.

that their fork springs notice the additional poundage of a light chair less, so there's little need to tamper with their springing. Martyn Aves, events manager of The Federation of Sidecar Clubs in Britain, wrote an article in *Outlook*, the club's magazine, in 2006, about this phenomenon: the unlikely ease with which modern cruisers harness up to sidecars. "When I chaired up," he wrote, having had a Squire RX4 put on his Yamaha XVS1100, "I was taken aback by how good the handling was. After all, I had made no modifications to the bike, yet it handled really well. It was frighteningly stable - you know the feeling: it's too good, something's wrong, it just doesn't work so easily first time."

All this, I know seems to fly in the face of the received wisdom of the ages, but I just don't think there's any need to modify the front end of a modern bike. If you leave it stock, you can revert quickly to solo use. If you feel you *must* fit leading-link forks, then try and get hold of Armec's gorgeous brushed alloy and gold forks - actually an adaptation of the Earles design. They are far more attractive, to my eyes at least, than the industrial, poking-forward, black bent-tubed affairs made by many British firms. Finally, if a little stiffening of the stock fork does seem necessary, what about a fork brace, like the Super Brace, available for Harleys and Metric bikes from the USA, fitted just above the mudguard?

Steering dampers

The central screw-down damper has gone completely. You would only find one of these on a classic design. Sometimes, you might feel the need to firm up the steering of your outfit, especially if it suffers from wheel-wobble on deceleration - a rare fault these days. If so you have three choices: fit wider handlebars, mount a lower-fork leg to sidecar-chassis damper, mount an upper fork-leg to bike-frame damper.

UNIT Sidecars hardly ever specify dampers. Their argument is that the rider's arms are the best dampers. This idea works when the handlebars are wide enough to give leverage. If your hands fall to the grips directly ahead of you, with arms parallel, then the bar is too short for chair work. Each arm should be positioned out from the straight-ahead by up to 30 degrees - 25 is fine. The sense of leverage and control over oscillation will feel very satisfactory.

Mounting a damper to your lower fork-leg is what Watsonian-Squire do if they feel you need it. A long-throw Volkswagen unit was the favourite. There are two drawbacks. The first is that if the damper acts so low on a single leg, it can encourage 'walking'. I remember on one bike I had, I could actually see the damped fork-leg bending against the damper relative to the other one. The other problem is that lock-to-lock turns are affected.

A most individual solution to the need for beefed-up rear suspension for a heavy chair. Double sprung dampers on this Honda in-line four and big Squire two-seat saloon sidecar. Note the solid steel car-wheel conversion which gives greater strength than spokes for the drive, and a smaller overall diameter also lowers the gearing.

Mounting a 'straight-through' damper, as fitted to some sports bikes with reduced trail to keep the steering steady, fitted between fork top and frame, is a better compromise. If the damper acts up near the top triple-tree the fork legs won't want to 'walk'.

Rear end suspension

As to the motorcycle's rear end, it is generally helpful to do one of two things. You can either adjust your single-shock or twin shocks (and such adjustments make far more of a difference now than they did on the primitive Armstrongs and Girlings of the '50s and '60s), or you can have them replaced.

Hagon's in the UK make replacement shocks for most modern bikes - and they feel just as nice for solo work when you take your chair off. Your sidecar supplier will fit these for you and it's well worth the labour cost, for it can be a fiddly job with those concealed spring 'hard-tail' look machines, and a nightmare with some big bodywork-encased tourers. This change of shock may almost certainly be the one useful adaptation you make because there is something disconcerting about the wallowy, 'sitting-down' sensation of too softly-sprung a bike and sidecar. You feel you're tipping over in turns into the chair, even though it's just the bike's rear squatting down.

It is worth working out what proportion of its weight a single-seat sidecar weighing 12 stone (one stone equals 14lbs) exerts on your bike. It's easy to do this. Put the bathroom scales under the chair's lower mounting arm, while supporting the front arm on a block. The bulk of the chair's weight will fall between its own wheel and the rear arm. That's as it should be. A nose-heavy chair can be dangerous, especially on turns away from the sidecar. The 9 stone left then divides between chair wheel and bike. So there's nothing like the weight of an adult pillion passenger on the rear end of the bike - so don't overdo the stiffer suspension, especially if you often ride alone. A sidecar's 'perceived' weight, as felt by the bike, has more to do with rolling friction, asymmetric posture and wind-resistance than its own *avoirdupois*.

Steering geometry and the mysteries of trail

Trail is the horizontal distance between the steering axis and a line from axle to the centre (strictly speaking the centroid) of the front tyre contact patch. Too much trail and the steering can be heavy, too little and things can get unstable. The concept of trail is illustrated opposite.

I mentioned earlier that the modern retro cruiser V-twin makes a surprisingly effective sidecar machine without much need for modification, particularly in the area of steering.

This Sunbeam S7 has standard forks with 4 or 5 inches of trail - the horizontal distance shown here

Centre of front tyre contact
patch

Steering axis

4-5 inches trail

This Triumph Bonneville has been fitted with leading link forks. Note how the front axle is mounted further in front of the line through the main bearing and thus gives zero trail at the centre of the tyre contact patch. Steering is light as a result.

Centre of front tyre contact patch and axis meet to give zero trail

The reasons for this lie in the geometry of tyre contact and trail. Vince Costa and Toph Bocchiaro, writing about optimal geometry, have pointed out that *both* front and rear wheels pivot about the steering axis and trail behind it. The steering axis, as we know, is not the line taken by the front forks – it is the line through the bearings in the steering head. A custom-style chopper with triple-trees pushed out to say 9 degrees would have the effect of creating a negative trail – equivalent to the axle of a castor on a tea-trolley getting stuck in front of its pivotal mounting. We know how it struggles to wobble round to get behind its vertical pivot line again. A front wheel under these conditions would be highly dangerous on a solo and, as pointed out in the 1960 edition of Iliffe's *Motorcycles And How To Manage Them*, '…even zero trail would only be suitable for a driver of immense experience because you cannot feel the sidecar at all'. But, mysteriously, old outfits with minimal to zero trail still seemed heavy to steer and wobbled, whereas modern ones with several inches of trail don't. What wasn't taken into account in the past was the angle of rear trail measured against the steering axis.

Below (left) this old Panther 650 has, with steering axis measured through the steering head bearings, zero trail, but the line of rear trail from steering head top to the centre of the rear tyre contact patch is several degrees below 90. By comparison (top) the same angle on this Yamaha is 90 degrees or more. And what makes the difference? Wheel base length. 1930s builders knew it by trial and error, but after WWII when ordinary solos with short wheel base were pressed into chair work, this vital parameter was neglected.

Centre of rear tyre contact patch. Angle here with the steering axis is greater than 90 degrees

Centre of front tyre contact patch

Steering axis

Line of rear trail to centre of rear tyre contact patch gives angle with the steering axis of less than 90 degrees

Steering axis (zero trail)

Springer front forks have a rigidity that telescopics can lack. Although not cheap (£1,000 at least, imported) they offer an attractive alternative to leading links. The action of a springer front fork, as in these Rolling Thunder US items, has the effect of putting the wheel axle ahead when the steering axis and vertical line at the centre of the tyre contact patch is measured. Trail is automatically reduced.

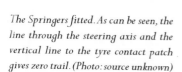

The Springers fitted. As can be seen, the line through the steering axis and the vertical line to the tyre contact patch gives zero trail. (Photo: source unknown)

These German Tornado touring outfits (above) have been extensively modified for big-mileage use. They have been fitted with small diameter car wheels and flat section tyres. Opinions about putting a flat tyre on the front of a trike or outfit vary. The turning action of forks automatically lifts a front tyre towards its sidewall, so many people think it makes sense to keep a standard round section tyre on the front of your conversion. There was recent correspondence about this in Motorcycle Sport and Leisure *concerning a BMW / Grinnall trike. The exception is where hub-centre steering has been fitted, as is the case on the BMW outfit on the right, where the front wheel is on a stub axle.*

Hub centre steering close-up (below) on an unidentified American outfit. The action of this method of steering is completely different to telescopic or leading link forks. As with a car, the wheel is turned on its stub axle at the hub, not from above. Clearly a flat section car tyre makes sense - although you could never use such a machine as a solo. Note how the leverage is led from above to the massive hub and how the huge combined spring and shock absorbers takes movement within its cradle, thus obviating the fork-dive so common with telescopics. Note the steering damper from chair frame to lower steering peg. (Photo courtesy of Russ Brown / Chuck Toro Attorneys))

Brakes

A fully floating front brake disc is often considered a worthwhile modification. All discs are very slightly gripped by the brake pads when the bike is in motion - that's why the discs feel warm even after little in the way of braking. On a sidecar outfit or trike fitted with conventional forks, if there is a slight flexure of the fork legs on corners, rigid disc brakes can rub or squeal against their pads. The calipers are fixed to the fork leg, but the axle carrying the disc may move a little out of line. Apart from being annoying - as all extraneous squeaks are - and virtually ineradicable, this causes more rapid brake-pad wear. When 4 or 6 pot calipers are employed, which naturally cover a large part of the disc's circumference, this sort of binding is even more likely.

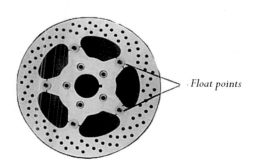

Float points

Floating discs eliminate all this. The braking surface only meets the wheel hub at 5 or 6 flexible points. The small amounts of fork flexure can be absobed by the play between the disc and the hub fitment. Many hard braking riders with heavy outfits generate a lot of heat in their discs. Floating discs do not pass this heat on to the wheel bearings.

Gearing changes: once *de rigeur*, now not so necessary

Another modification which was deemed vital in the old days was a change from solo to sidecar gearing. This was usually achieved by bolting on a larger rear gear-sprocket and adding links to the chain. I agree that it was necessary with singles in particular, and I certainly had it done (by adopting a smaller drive sprocket) when I used chain-driven singles on chairs. It is, however, another of those necessities from the past whose days have gone. The torque from engines commonly in the region of 1500cc and the widespread adoption of shaft- or belt-drive on most cruisers, nature's obvious sidecar pullers, make any attempt to alter the stock gearing impracticable and unnecessary. I quizzed an engineer at Watsonian-Squire about this when they were first offering a complete combination of cruiser and chair. He thought there was no need to make changes at all because of the immense strength of the wet multi-plate clutches on modern machines and the sophistication of electronic engine-mapping systems. For those who need infinitely flexible gearing, however, there is the astonishing development by Mobec of Germany of the 'Duo-Drive' and 'Super-Drive' which can take power out from the bike to an under-chair floor box via an electronic selector which can give 12 forward and 12 reverse gears and drive through visco-hydraulic converters to chair wheel and bike front wheel, if desired. Where a serious long-distance touring outfit is intended, some get their builder to replace the bike's original wheels with smaller car-type steel ones, thus lowering the gearing. In most cases no change will need to be made to the speedometer, and it isn't easy to alter electronic ones.

A vague association of sidecars with the classic bike movement has continued to perpetuate several of the old absolutes of the mid-20th century sidecar man. If one is running an outfit based on an old BSA A10 or Panther 120, with contact-breaker ignition, dry clutch and less than 40lb-ft of torque available, then such absolutes may well apply. However, David Minton, whose wise words I have quoted already, pointed out, in a chapter about sidecars in *The Motorcyclist's Handbook* published in 1981, that without one or all of the modifications referred to above (fork substitution, reduced trail, tyre change, lowered gearing) "an inferior, although possibly acceptable, performance is guaranteed". He hasn't changed his mind; in *RealClassic* magazine (June 2008) he wrote: "Do not believe anyone, not even third-wheel traders, who tell you that down-gearing is unnecessary with outfits. It's vital." Given the difficulties and expense of changing gearing with shafties or belt-driven bikes, I guess the sensible thing to do is choose a slightly under-geared machine in the first place, and for this a test drive is what's really vital.

Sidecar brakes

Merlin Sidecars supply their chairs with hydraulic discs; Watsonian-Squire and UNIT don't automatically recommend them, but have drum-braked wheels available if needed. The simplest are cable-operated by a pedal on the chair frame, but if the chair is on the left, this suits the classic bike best, with its left-foot brake and right-foot gear lever. Braking a chair helps swing the bike round on turns into the sidecar, of course, but modern bikes' stoppers are so strong that an additional one on a decently weighted sidecar is by no means a necessity to bring it to a halt.

Extreme modifications for performance sidecarring

If you go to the far, far edge of performance sidecarring on the road, you can, in addition to the modifications above, route your oil via an outboard cooler in the wind between sidecar and bike, add compressed-air programmable ride-stiffening and posture via the chair's suspension (in the USA at least), and enclose the whole plot in wind-cheating fibre-glass. It will, naturally, go very fast, look astounding and cost a fortune. Such modifications won't, however, enable you to pop your chair on and off at will and use your bike any way you wish.

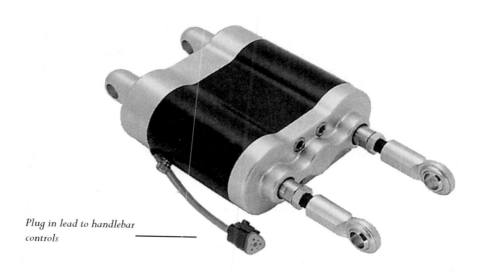

Plug in lead to handlebar
controls

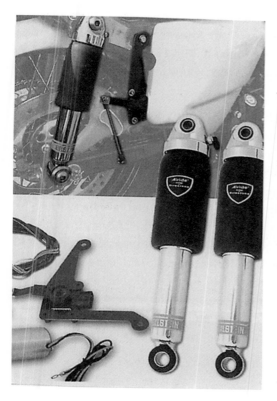

Examples of air-adjustable shocks. Unlike programmable shocks which need a tweak with a tool, these devices are actuated from the handle-bar. Compressors raise or lower and stiffen or soften at will. Top is a Custom Cycle unit for concealed 'soft tail' bikes with internal pump and dump valve (about £800 imported). Below are some Firestone air-rides with Bilstein shocks from Alloy Art in America, complete with onboard compressor and ECU sensor intended for twin rear damper bikes. In America, air-adjustable suspension is common on sidecars - a smooth ride is all! (Photo courtesy of Alloy Art)

PREPARING AND DRIVING YOUR CONVERSION

Trikes

There is a lot more mystique around the piloting of a sidecar outfit than there is around trikes. It is almost sufficient, when discussing trikes, to recommend (a) going round corners fairly slowly and (b) remembering that there is a lot of width behind you. Car-based trikes are low with long wheelbases. They squat down hard and heavy, and they have wide rear tracks. You sit within them, also low down. They won't have the same tendency to lift an inside wheel as the higher, short-wheelbase bike conversion upon which you are perched. I prefer the latter for all the reasons I have given, but care is required. Reading the road surface is as important as it is on a solo; the triple track finds it harder to miss holes and bumps than a twin- or single-track vehicle. Gently does it until you are on the highway.

You do see trikes fitted with dampers, but steering is heavy enough on a trike without one of these. Because of the equal distribution of power, brakes and steering, there is no difference between a left- and right-hand corner, other than that imposed by the road's camber. There is nothing to be gained by altering throttle position according to the corner. On a trike it is best to maintain a steady speed in corners; the trick being to have arrived at the corner at the correct speed in the first place. The great difference between a VW car-based rear-engined trike, with its low centre of gravity and 80/20 ratio of weight and braking rear/front, and a bike-based conversion which will typically have a 55/45 rear/front ratio means that they handle markedly differently. The bike-conversion wheels have roughly equal weight on them, the engine's mass being cradled between the three. This does have implications for cornering - the bike-conversion has much less of a sled/dragster profile and can't be chucked into corners quite so readily. However, once in them, the front wheel is less likely to break away and lose grip, especially in the wet.

Sidecars

Once upon a time - somewhere between 1920 and 1964 - men who rode motorcycles knew how to control sidecar outfits. Today a biker will go his whole motoring life and never experience the maddening, but inexplicably fascinating challenge of piloting a chair.

Assuming you haven't fixed the sidecar on yourself, but had it fitted by one of the specialists who sold it to you, you shouldn't have too much fettling to do when you get it home - although it would be surprising if you had to do nothing at all. Sidecarring is a rather personal thing because tiny adjustments make such *huge* differences in the pleasure, or otherwise, of driving. Until you've got it just right, you will find yourself endlessly re-aligning, tightening and slackening. I would be surprised if you were not plagued by a maddening creak or squeak; sidecar outfits are prone to these. A couple of years ago I nearly went insane trying to cure what I thought was a suspension squeal. I greased and oiled, disassembled and re-assembled, and had friends travel in the chair trying to pinpoint the exact location. I fiddled with the bike's suspension, its driveline and every part of the sidecar chassis and fitments. The noise was eventually traced to a single loose bolt holding the chair's front end onto its frame, and I only discovered this when the chair was off for a service and the thing squeaked as I lifted it.

Those old parameters

If you have decided to attach the sidecar yourself, you need to bear in mind the few 'rules' to which I referred earlier. The chair needs to be a little 'pigeon-toed' in relation to the bike's wheels, so the nose of the chair has to be an inch or two in towards the front of the bike, not absolutely parallel. They used to recommend using straight planks against the motorcycle wheels to determine this, but as nearly all machines have unequal width tyres nowadays, this isn't much of a guide. Once the outfit is running, you will soon know if you've got it right. If the whole vehicle has a tendency to pull towards the kerb, you need to increase the 'toe-in' a little more and reduce it if it pulls towards the off-side.

The motorcycle's 'lean-out' from bolt upright is not something which was considered necessary at the beginning of the age of biking. In 1912, I was interested to learn, the prevailing advice was to ensure that bike wheels and sidecar wheel were exactly parallel, both horizontally and vertically. Presumably, experience in use on progressively faster machines brought about the now universal agreement that 'lean-out' is as important as 'toe-in'. About an inch and a half should be enough. As I've said already, you'll know when it's right - and there's quite a lot of fun to be had from experimenting.

Whether your sidecar has been attached by you, following the purchase of clamps, bolts, lugs and tubes from one of the firms referred to earlier, or whether you've let one of them fit it for you, you will eventually want to make fine adjustments to suit your own riding conditions, your weight and what the outfit will be carrying. A socket set is going to be a necessity. Furthermore, all sidecar fitments require periodic re-tightening - especially where clamps alone are used.

Lead rolls: a neat sort of ballast

If you usually carry a passenger, your chair should feel balanced. If it doesn't, and the whole plot seems to want to drag to the near-side, it's because 'toe-in' or 'lean-out' are not quite right. If you mainly drive the combo on your own, you will need some ballast to simulate load. The old suggestion of a bag of sand on the seat isn't very practical; you wouldn't be able to give anyone a lift, and it might burst. The best weighting material is soft lead, available in rolls from builder's merchants.

This can be used to line the sidecar boot and the under-seat area; and it's best to keep the ballast over the sidecar wheel and bike's rear axle, rather than in its nose. Too heavy a nose can lead to the danger of tipping on turns away from the chair. If the bike's rear wheel should lift in mid-corner, anything could happen. Also, it's best, especially if using stock forks, to keep load on them as light as is practicable. But the most delightful sidecarring is done with a chair which doesn't encumber the bike too much, so you should try to keep the overall ballast as light as you can. Because the weight is most effective when it's furthest from the bike, try rolling the sheet lead into thin bars, sealing them in gaffer tape, and then placing a few of them under the seat nearest to the sidecar wheel or against the boot's near-side wall. About 3 stone of lead roll placed like this is more effective than 6 stone of it under the carpet. The addition of a passenger on occasion then won't seem like quite such a big load. The aim of all this is to let the sidecar suspension and bike rear suspension compress together when meeting bumps. An outfit can seem horribly jiggly if the sidecar is bouncing up and down next to a more softly suspended machine. Properly weighted, with adjustments judiciously made, a balanced combo should float along the road. One of the most striking characteristics of sidecar outfits is the vast difference between one that is properly set-up, aligned and weighted and one that isn't. Aching shoulders and uneasy feelings of imbalance bedevil the latter; effortless security and precision reward the former.

Steering an outfit

All solo bikers lean on bends, so it's a shock to realise that, apart from Flexit or Armec style 'leaners', you have to steer a rigid outfit using the bars as a tiller, taking deliberate turns to right or left. That's why it pays to have wide handlebars, as standard on American-styled cruisers. Generally the outfit will go where you point it, but there is a difference between left- and right-hand turns because most of the weight, all the drive, all the braking (unless you have a sidecar brake) and all the steering is on one side of the vehicle. Taking a bend into the sidecar (a left turn in Britain) is the one which novices fear most. The sidecar's wheel will seem to be trying to lift, and a natural reaction is to cut speed to get it down again. It's worth remembering three things: firstly, the wheel may not be lifting at all - the bike will be squatting on its suspension while the chair wheel's suspension is slackening; secondly, you'd have to be going very fast actually to tip the whole thing over - so that's not likely, however much it may feel as if it's imminent; lastly, a twist of the throttle half-way through the bend when you can see the exit will drive the bike round the un-powered sidecar wheel. If you can brake your chair as well, the bike will swing even more easily round it. It upsets the line-up of your outfit if you decelerate in mid-curve, so you need to practice not doing this and taking both left- and right-handers gently - if only for the well-being of your spokes, forks and bearings.

On turns away from the sidecar (a right turn in Britain), it is the bike which needs to slow, so that it becomes the fulcrum around which the sidecar travels. Deceleration and a gentle touch of brake help the outfit round. These turns always feel more secure because the sidecar is supporting the bike. When you can see the bend's exit, just open up again.

Magazines from the 1920s to the '60s often show sidecar pilots and their passengers leaning dramatically left and right as they corner. There's no doubt that this sort of weight transference can help if you're cornering fast in a race, but on the road it always seems sufficient just to sit comfortably upright, resisting the centrifugal forces as the expert sidecarrist Vic Willoughby recommended, by pressure of the knee on the tank.

Speed humps

When sidecar wheels drop into dips in the road they have the effect of momentarily jerking the outfit out of line into the chair. Sleeping policemen or speed-humps can do the same. It's a good tip to read the road surface and avoid potholes and dropped manhole covers, and when approaching speed-humps which run across the road to do so at a slight angle. This will have the effect of bringing your chair wheel and bike rear wheel to the hump at the same time. Remember that your sidecar wheel has a 'lead' of 6 to 9 inches.

As I've mentioned already, the bike's handlebars may want to oscillate when decelerating or meeting irregularities, 'head-waggling' as the old-timers called it. And as I have explained earlier, the fitting of a damper will stop this, although some firms find that such a device is never required. If the road surface is studied and the outfit guided to ride out deviations, or to avoid them, there won't be a problem.

Modern bikes have very beefy front forks which don't seem affected by either the weight or the steering stresses of a sidecar. Leaving the bike stock means that it can easily be used as a solo when the chair is slipped off - and even more easily re-sold. (Photo courtesy Watsonian-Squire)

Watsonian, who made a post-war in-house 1000ccV-twin prototype outfit using a JAP engine, were content with telescopics. The venture did not get beyond this one machine, because JAP were unwilling to supply a small order for their motors. The combo (featuring an early Avon part glass-fibre chair, and painted in mist green favoured for '50s Sunbeams and the BSA Bantam) is in the National Motorcycle Museum.

COMBOS AND TRIKES IN THE PRESS

As the powered trike is a fairly new phenomenon in Britain, it hasn't had much long-term press exposure. There are magazines which, to date, have been the natural home of the trike fancier, particularly *Back Street Heroes (BSH)*, published in London, and, most recently, *Trike*, available from Jazz Publishing via the Internet. The main thrust of *BHS* is the one-off custom bike scene, but there's always a bit of coverage about trikes, mainly in the form of photos of machines seen at custom shows. The trike makers advertise at the back too, although as the tone of the mag is more biker-society gossip than technical review, there's not much detailed engineering discussed. *Trike* has articles about the major trike builders, as well as reviews of their products and coverage of the sort of one-off custom creations which feature so widely in American magazines.

Very, very rarely the mainstream bike press runs a short article about a triked motorcycle - but so infrequently that I can only bring to mind three or four in the past five years: a review of a Honda Valkyrie trike done in the USA, a review of the Martin-Conquest for wheelchair-bound drivers - both these in that most eclectic of magazines, *Motorcycle Sport and Leisure* - and a couple of articles in *The Classic Motorcycle*, one on the Moto Guzzi 'Mule' army trike and the other on a restored Harley-Davidson Servicar. As I have intimated already, trikes aren't big enough in the UK as yet to warrant column inches.

The history of the sidecar combination in Britain's motorcycling press has had a much more interesting ride. In the great sidecar heyday, between the early '50s and mid-'60s, the two titles *Motorcycling* and *The Motor Cycle* gave vast amounts of space to the design, advertising and application of outfits. *Motorcycle Mechanics* ran article after article, week after week, full of advice about construction, maintenance, control on the road and purchase. These examples are typical:

Motorcycling

05/1951	Vincent Rapide and Blacknell Sherwood.
04/1958	BSA Golden Flash and Watsonian Avon.
06/1958	Velocette Venom and Steib.
02/1959	Triumph Tiger and Wessex.

The Motor Cycle

11/1956	Sidecars for 1957.
08/1957	Test of Royal Enfield Super Meteor and Garrard chair.
11/1960	Sidecar Show.
03/1962	'A Monza Takes Its Medicine'; test on a Velo Viper and RE 700.
11/1962	12 adverts for sidecars

Motorcycle Mechanics

07/1960	21 hints for sidecar owners.
01/1961	Sidecar maintenance & buyers' guide to 1961 chairs.
11/1961	Building a sidecar.
02/1962	Improving a sidecar.
05/1962	Choosing a chair.
09/1962	Editorial about sidecars for learners.
03/1964	Panther combo test & control a chair.
07/1967	BSA/Watsonian Monza super test.
11/1969	How to handle 3 wheels.

As the fifties drew to a close, the motorcycle dealers, like Elite of Tooting and Pride and Clarke began to advertise Ford 'Pop' cars, Minis and Morris Minors among the second-hand sidecar combinations; the mayfly-like golden era was suddenly over. There is virtually no mention of sidecar outfits in the motorcycling press of the '70s and early '80s. Manufacturers assumed that chairs would no longer be fitted to their bikes, and most, as I have explained elsewhere, discouraged the practice.

Magazines today

Then - like the first flutterings of an osprey chick which shows that the species has been brought back from the edge of extinction - articles, references and reminiscences began to appear once again in magazines.

'Classic' magazines in the UK

The Classic Motorcycle, founded and edited by the late, great Bob Currie, started some balls rolling. In Issue no. 2 (Aug/Sept 1981) there were 11 pictures of sidecar outfits, some historical, which out of 74 visual images is a fair percentage.

This trend in *The Classic Motorcycle* continued rapidly, and adverts appeared from the mid- to late-1980s for that old faithful Watsonian, for the products of UNIT and of Charnwood, so that once again it was possible to purchase from a choice of new sidecars other than the right-hand fitting products of the USSR and its satellites.

The Classic Motorcycle has featured well over 60 sidecar outfits on every imaginable bike between 1985 and 2005. In 240 editions, over a quarter of these has a sidecar article. Motorcycles featured have included Ariel, Enfield, Ural, the ultra-rare Brough 4, Clyno, Premier, Benelli, Douglas, Moto Guzzi, Matchless, Zundapp, BMW, Vindec, Scott, Vincent, BSA, FN, Rudge, Sunbeam S7, MZ, Triumph, Velocette, Norton, Motobecane, Rex, Auto Cycle Union, Puch and Harley - all in harness with sidecars large and small. There have also been focus articles on sidecar makers like Steib, Canterbury, Watsonian, Charnwood, Swallow and VP; and one delightful issue (Sept 1989) which was entitled 'A Sidecar Extravaganza' and featured a group of outfits in a giant test.

Classic Bike, *Classic Bike Guide*, the ephemeral *Motorcycle Classics* and latterly *Real Classic* have all followed suit, giving sidecar coverage very much greater than ownership, on the road, seems to merit.

Classic Bike had articles about combos in April '85, May '85, March '87, October '87, including a series about Watsonian's history and their rally, and from then on outfits appeared regularly: Triumph Thunderbird and Palma (Feb '96), Velocette combo (Feb '94), BSA AA outfit (Sept '93), BSA taxi outfits in Indonesia (June '94), Indian outfits (Aug '94), Panther 120 combo (Mar '03), A7 and Garrard (April '93), Harley outfit (March '93), A65 and Steib (Nov '92), OEC outfit, Norton outfit & Ariel outfits (Jun '92) to name just a few.

Classic Bike Guide featured a BSA M21 and chair and a French Vannod chair in July '06, BMW & Panther 120 sidecar tugs in Sept '01, MZ 500 and chair (Aug '94), A5 and chair (May '03) and lots of nostalgic street scenes with Busmar Astral and other combinations in evidence.

Real Classic, a recent subscription-only publication, had an AJS outfit in April '06, an EML outfit in May '06 and an article on sidecar gearing in June '08.

Motorcycle Sport and Leisure, the best of the 'modern scene' quality magazines, has featured the BMW 1100GS and chair (July '99), a Honda Blackbird outfit (May '99), a Triumph and Flexit (Nov '93), Ural and chair (May 2000), and Ural again (July 2000), a Triumph Triple hearse (Feb '03), a BSA and Steib (Nov '06), a DragStar and Watsonian GP700 (Feb '08) and a two-part Enfield/Watsonian winter trip to Scotland (June & July '08) and a Ural 'gear-up' (Dec '08). Their recently introduced small ads pages had three outfits and a sidecar for sale in May 2008 two outfits and two trikes in November 2008 and a trike and a chair in December 2008.

So there is a wealth of interesting archive material to delve into in these past copies - all of which supports the notion that while you may not often *see* a sidecar outfit on the streets, there is still an interest in reading about them. I guess it's akin to detective/murder novels. One seldom, if ever, actually murders people oneself or discovers who did so by detection, but one likes to read about those who do.

Specialist sidecar magazines

Overseas, there are some specialist magazines devoted entirely to sidecars, in particular *Gespanne* in Germany and *Hack'd* in the USA. *Gespanne* is an advertising supported, glossy magazine devoted entirely to sidecars whilst *Hack'd* is more in the style of a club magazine, primarily subscription based but still completely devoted to sidecars.

Modern bike magazines

By contrast, it is noticeable that that section of the motorcycle press which supports and encourages fast sports bike riders *never* mentions sidecar use. Clearly, in spite of the existence of Charnwood, Merlin *et al*, and the long tradition of the sports combo in Britain, sidecars are not seen as compatible with whatever statement one makes when buying a 150bhp sports replica and doing wheelies on it.

The dominant tone - one might perhaps call it the pose - taken by contributors on sidecar matters over the past ten years or so, is one of alarmed caution. When about to write a review of an outfit, they approach the machine with timidity, reiterating all the old saws about not letting the chair-wheel lift on left-handers, not letting the bike's wheel lift on right-handers, coping with steering wobble, and slipping the clutch to get away. They are generally 'converted' by the end of the article - but never whole-heartedly so. When their turn comes to ride in the chair, they are deafened by the proximity of the bike, shaken by the potholes in the road and alarmed by vegetation and street furniture which is invariably described as 'whipping past my left ear'. Sometimes they shut their eyes as their pilot swings them from corner to corner. The general impression left by such reportage is that sidecar ownership is for the faintly lunatic, the eccentric's choice - a not very *pleasant* thing to do, if fascinating. The written style of such articles (with the great exceptions of Jonathan Jones and Philip Tooth) is wryly humorous.

This may well account for the smallish number of people who go in for sidecar driving. It once seemed to be up (or down) there with Morris Dancing, even in that section of the motorcycling press most prone to feature it, and the 1990s *Two Fat Ladies* and *Wallace and Gromit* phenomena managed to add a further veil of the ribald over the whole thing.

But that attitude seems to have faded away and sidecars are now seen as the (slightly eccentric, perhaps) leisure pursuit of a few, but now with less of the old cartoon images associated with them.

Books on sidecars and trikes

There are very few books in English about the phenomenon of the sidecar attachment, and only one that I know of about triking, *Three Wheelers - The Complete History of Trikes 1885 - 1995* by Chris Rees, (ISBN 1 899814 05 1). Martin Franitza has written in German about outfits but has not been fully translated, nor have one or two short Japanese works.

Jo Axon wrote *Our Sidecars* in 1988 (ISBN 0 9515702 0 X) but this is now out of print, and there is a little Shire Books pamphlet called *Sidecars* from the same author, published in 1996 and now into a second edition. *Our Sidecars* is dated, referring to the late '70s / early '80s sidecar scene in Britain. Some of the firms it details have long since ceased trading and a lot of its advice assumes home-building and fitting which is less likely in these days of greater affluence. It needed detailed editing too and its mistakes of style and punctuation make it an annoying read; although it remains, of course, of interest to the sidecar fancier. The Shire book has been edited thoroughly, but is very limited in scope because of its size.

Geoff Brazendale's *The Sidecar - a History* came out in 1999 (ISBN 0 9534961 0 4) and, as far as I am aware, is still available. This is a thorough investigation into the growth of the combination from the beginning of the 20th century and contains an encyclopaedia of most (but not all) firms which manufactured them. This is a handsome, large-format, hard-back 'coffee-table' book and well worth acquiring.

Richard and Mopsa English wrote *Full Circle: Around the World with a Motorcycle and Sidecar,* a very readable and charming 1980s account of their four year round-the-world epic ride on a Meriden Triumph 650 with Squire sidecar (ISBN 085429662 X). Their outfit, incidentally is preserved in the National Motorcycle Museum.

John Procter wrote *Watsonian Sidecars* for that firm's 75th anniversary in the mid '80s, and, finally, Jeff Clew's *Motorcycling in the '50s* (ISBN 1 874105 46 4) from 1995 contains an entertaining chapter entitled: *'Whatever happened to the sidecar?'*

The world's oldest sidecar: the 1903 Graham Brothers Patent Sociable

IN CONCLUSION

You could be lucky, as I once was, and find that a TV company wishes to hire your combo or trike for a documentary or film. You could test your endurance to the limit and go on winter events like the Elephant or Dragon Rally. In every country there are organisations that you can join, like the Federation of Sidecar Clubs in the UK, and a host of one-make groups, such as The Hedingham Owners Club. A main interest of their members is getting together, often on camp-sites, and partying in olde-worlde style. *Outlook,* the magazine of the Fed, sometimes bemoans the low attendance at some of these parties, and I can understand why. It's not everyone who enjoys tents, with their suggestion of 'Carry On Camping', and communal latrines. It is possible that even the possessors of trikes and outfits have moved on psychologically from 1960's notions of leisure time. Perhaps they should follow the classic car movement and organise trips based around four-star hotels and stately homes. Until then, participation may not suit everyone.

Many words have been written about 'demoting your bike' to sidecar haulage, about 'taming the wild beast by harnessing it to a chair', about sidecar machines being 'dull plodders'. One sees the point. If you have a conventionally-designed, reasonably-priced sidecar attached simply and handily to your stock bike, you are not going to be able to go as fast as you would without it. There - it's said. Far-edge outfits apart, the three-wheeler is just too ungainly, asymmetric, un-aerodynamic and ornery a brute to risk at very high speeds - except perhaps in a straight line. But I'd like to enthuse again about what many solo bikers would consider to be a perverse slowness.

Clearly, we are never going to return to the days when, as Thomas Hardy put it, 'England is a continent'. And it would be pointless not to get to places in *reasonable* time, but I don't think enough is made of that 'nirvana' state of having plenty of time, of never needing to rush, of having spare engine power and torque and not having to use it, and thus travelling in the sure knowledge that you will not break down because you don't strain your machine, that if someone steps out, or a car crosses your path you can calmly avoid them, braking with space to spare. This is all possible with a trike or a sidecar outfit because you are licensed by public expectation of your speed and by the forces of gravity.

You commence your ride in a frame of mind enhanced by the knowledge that you are aboard a vehicle which has exerted a particular and endless fascination. A glance through Geoff Brazendales's *The Sidecar - a History* will reveal over 350 makes of sidecar which have bobbed up in the past hundred years or so since the Sangsters started making the *Liberty Sociable* from the Graham Brothers' patent in 1903. No less astonishing is a flip through the internet sites connected with sidecars and trikes. The guy in the street who gazes after your outfit almost certainly imagines that sidecars exist only in museums. Being accorded a different status from ordinary motorists and motorcyclists, you can behave differently, occupying a unique bubble of identity, time and space for as long as you are at the helm of your machine.

The decision to pay for that third wheel goes back fundamentally to what I discussed at the beginning. It is a need to step back from the dangers of solo riding and its competitiveness in today's demanding traffic conditions, but still being in the open air; it's a fondness for an arcane expression of difference in an ocean of sameness; it's an affinity for simple mechanics and it is the pleasure that comes from mastering a challenging vehicle under all circumstances. If even one of these imperatives is unappealing then it's unlikely that you will go any further towards ownership than reading magazine articles or books like this. But if what I have written strikes a chord, then you will not regret purchasing that fascinating, if eccentric, accessory - a third wheel.

Sidecar combinations catch the eye - especially if there's a dog on board - as here in this Coop advertisement in the street outside a shop in Switzerland.

SIDECAR AND TRIKE CONTACTS

SIDECAR MANUFACTURERS AND SUPPLIERS

UK

Charnwood Classic Restorations
own make and second-hand sidecars,
fitting service

(+44) 01530832634

www.charnwoodclassic.com

F2 Motorcycles
importers of Ural outfits and Velorex
sidecars and fittings

(+44) 01295712900

www.f2motorcycles.ltd.uk

Ural outfit in the woods. (Photo F2 Motorcycles)

Beautiful Merlin sidecar. (Photo courtesy of Merlin Sideacrs)

Merlin Sidecars   (+44) 01913866777   www.merlinsidecars.co.uk
sidecars, fitting service

Unit Sidecars Ltd   (+44) 01787461000   www.unitsidecars.co.uk
makers of Hedingham sidecars, leading link
forks and fitments

Wasp   (+44) 01722792827   wasp-motorcycles.tripod.com
manufacturers of pre 1985 trials
competition chairs

Watsonian-Squire Ltd   (+44) 01386701162   www.watsonian-squire.com
large range of sidecars, fittings,
importers of Royal Enfield

Europe

Armec (Switzerland)   –   www.armec.com
leaning and conventional sidecars;
also in USA

EML (Holland)   (+31) 0545292154   www.emlsidecar.com
sidecar and trike engineers and suppliers

EZS (Holland)   (+31) 0314621849   www.ezs-sidecar.com
luxury sidecars, fitting kits

Ideal-seitenwagen (Germany) –   www.ideal-seitenwagen.de
replica Steib sidecars and spares

India

Cozy Sidecars   (+91) 1128751080
traditional Indian-made all-steel chairs

Cozy Sidecars (Canada)   (+1) 8002018110   www.cozysidecar.ca

Cozy Sidecars (USA)   (+1) 8002017472   www.enfieldmotorcycles.com

China

Chang Jiang   –   www.chinasidecars.cm
replica BMW outfits and chairs   jbzhang750@g.mail.com

USA

California Sidecars   (+1) 8008241523   www.californiasidecar.com
stylish sporty sidecars

Champion Sidecars   (+1) 7148470949   www.championsidecars.com
bikes, trailers, chairs, special steering and
reverse kits

Dauntless Motors   (+1) 3608254610   www.dauntlessmotors.com
sophisticated, advanced sidecars

Hannigan Sidecars   (+1) 2707534256   www.hannigansidecar.com
striking, advanced sports chairs

Motorvation   (+1) 8003053664   www.motorvation.com
range of chairs

Texas Sidecars   (+1) 9036402149   www.texassidecars.com
low, single-seat chairs

Action shot of a Watsonian-Squire GP700 in Jubilee trim teamed up with a Yamaha XVS 1100A and sold up to 2008 by Watsonian as a matched outfit with firm's warranty (photo courtesy Watsonian-Squire)

TRIKE MANUFACTURERS AND SUPPLIERS

Trike Builders

UK

Baron Trikes   (+44) 01264353571   www.barontrikes.co.uk
all fibre-glass bodywork for Harley,
Honda and Victory trikes

BB Customs   (+44) 0120289 0680   www.bbcustoms.biz
Harley conversions with special chain-
drive differential

Boss Hoss in the UK   (+44) 01344779000   www.bosshossmotorcycles.co.uk
for V8 Chevy-powered 2 & 3 wheelers

C&C Trikes   (+44) 01622817703   www.candcmc.co.uk
specialise in shaft-driven conversions
with Wolfrace wheels

Diamond Trikes   (+44) 02838852635   www.diamondtrikes.co.uk

Edinburgh Trike Services   (+44) 0131 6651822 www.edinburghtrikeservices.co.uk
makes a change from Wales or the
West Country!

Eurotech   (+44) 01424444349   www.eurotech-trikes.co.uk
wide range of designs

Grinnall Cars   (+44) 01299822862   www.grinnallcars.com
three-wheeled cars and trike conversions
including the newly launched R3T, a
Triumph Rocket 3 based conversion

*Left, BMW 1200 boxer seamlessly converted by Grinnall into a very pretty trike. Note the provision of a handbrake -
a requirment on a trike in British law. Right, by contrast this almost skeletal conversion by Rhino Trikes of a Suzuki
1400 Intruder V-twin is an excellent example of the airy lightness which can be achieved.*

Nice example of a Wildcat Trike (Photo Wildcat Trikes)

Harley-Davidson UK   (+44) 08709041450   www.harley-davidson.com
in 2009 the new TrGlide trike is available
from dealers

Lightning Custom Engineering   (+44) 01472399899   -
full- and part-builds and parts

Martin Conquest   (+44) 01613510324   www.martinconquest.co.uk
BMW adaptations for wheel-chair driving

Pro Custom   (+44) 01709555717   www.procustom.co.uk
Yorkshire based trike specialists

Rhino Trikes   (+44) 0146030170   www.rhino-trikes.co.uk
Suzuki Intruder conversions

TAB Customs   (+44) 01302832600   www.tab-customs.com
specialises in DragStar trikes

Trike Design   (+44) 02920880885   www.hankschopshop.com
famous trike builders and designers of
chain-drive and reverse systems;
Lehman importers

The Trike Shop   (+44) 02920369420   www.trikeshop.co.uk
long-established builder and kit supplier
of high quality

Trikemaster   (+44) 08702325555   www.welovebikes.co.uk
will build trikes up to 7 seats using
Ford components

United Trikes   (+44) 01626360819   www.unitedtrikes.com
bespoke conversions

Wackey's Trikes all machines triked to a very high standard; attractive ancillaries	(+44) 01837659612	www.wackeystrikes.co.uk
Wildcat Trikes Chris Spalding Engineering Rover 114 auto-based trikes	(+44) 01476572028	www.wildcatrikes.co.uk

UK importers and agents

Colin Appleyard Motorcycles Ltd importers of Lehman and EML trike conversions of Honda GoldWings	(+44) 08456447835 (+44) 01535606311	www.colinappleyard.co.uk
Boom Trikes (UK) importers of the German range of Boom Trikes	(+44) 01617997103	www.boom-trikes.co.uk
MBT Customs importers of Rewaco rear-engined trikes	(+44) 01392825687	www.mbtcustoms.co.uk
Pump Action importers of the Can-Am Spyder	(+44) 01778341144	www.pumpaction.co.uk
UK Triker Shop suppliers of Boom, Rewaco and other VW based trikes	(+44) 01159750880	www.uktriker.co.uk

Europe importers and agents

Piaggio three-wheeled scooters	**contact nearest dealer** 0080081829800	www.ukpiaggio.com
TrikeTec German Tiptronic/automatic trikes with servicing points in the UK	(+49) 07634552630	www.triketec.com
V12 Trikes	–	www.v12-trikes.de

Boom Trikes Low Rider 6i Classic. (Photo Boom Trikes)

Boss Hoss winged trike makes a stunning machine! (Photo courtesy Boss Hoss Cycles)

USA & Canada

Better'n'most Trikes
make sidecars and trikes
(+1) 860623 2547
www.sidecar.com

Boss Hoss
world's largest motorcycles and
bike-based trikes
–
www.bosshoss.com

BRP
comprehensive website for the Spyder trike
–
www.BRP.com

Dauntless Motors
trike kits for Honda VTX, GoldWing
& Yamaha Road Star
(+1) 3608254610/5446
www.dauntlessmotors.com

Ecstasy Cycles
make Renegade V8 trikes
(+1) 8885886405
www.renegadetrikes.com

Kopavi trikes
(+1) 4063630514
www.kopavi.com

Lightning
(+1) 8669991958
www.lightningmotorcycles.com

Metal Magic
(+1) 6023040404
www.metalmagic.com

Motor Trike
stylish Victory, H/D and Honda
conversions
(+1) 9038423094
www.motortrike.com

Nova Trikes
Alabama based Harley-Davidson and
BMW conversions
(+1) 256230 0300
www.novatrikes.com

Tri King
Florida-based Honda GoldWing
trike makers
(+1) 386334 0519
www.trikingtrikes.com

| Tri Wing | (+1) 250658 8475 | www.triwing.com |
| Vigillante
for the Tri-vette kit | (+1) 3172873232 | www.vigillante.com |

Trike and outfit hire

| Dragonride
UK hire firm | (+44) 07840760394 | www.dragonride.org.uk |
| Moto Provencale Ltd
French based Ural outfit holiday hire | (+33) 432601566 | www.sidecarholidays.com |

Trike transporter makers

| Trail-a-trike
for transporting your trike | (+44) 01158773770 | www.trike-register.co.uk |

PARTS AND ACCESSORIES

Alloy Art air-adjustable shocks and suspension accessories	(+1) 6269365021	www.alloyart.com
AMS Custom Cycles wide range of custom needs	(+44) 01752848223	www.amscustomcycles.com
Compomotive Wheels motorsport lightweight wheels for cars and trikes	(+44) 01902311499	www.compo.co.uk
Custom Cruisers vast range of accessories	(+44) 01773835666	www.customcruisers.co.uk
Custom Works Parts for Harley-Davidsons	(+1) 3862571300	www.customworksdaytona.com
Doctor DragStar beefier sounding pipes for Yamaha Stars through surgery	(+44) 01484455978	www.flitwickmotorcycles.co.uk
Hagon shocks suppliers of shock absorbers & suspension for conversions	(+44) 02085026222	www.hagon-shocks.co.uk
Harrison Billet high quality brake systems	(+44) 01795477752	www.billet.co.uk
Highway Hawk Dutch supplier of vast range of accessories for all makes, esp. cruisers	(+31) 0342490208	www.highwayhawk.com
Jardine motorcycle exhausts	(+1) 9517395900	www.jardineproducts.com
JP Cycles American suppliers of air-shocks, Harley-Davidson and metric parts	(+1) 8003974844	www.jpcycles.com

An eccentric accessory. A box sidecar on a Virago makes for an unusual outfit these days.
(Photo courtesy Watsonian-Squire)

Kliktronic   (+44) 01359242100   www.kliktronic.co.uk
importers of the Scandinavian handle-bar
mounted gear-change system. NABD approved

Mobec   (+49) 0716132141   www.mobec.de
German manufacturers of advanced
sidecar gearbox and drive systems

Motorcycle Voyager   (+44) 07828162016   www.mtcvoyager.com
US manufacturers of outrigger   j.davidson1@sky (in the UK)
wheels for most big bikes. UK contact

Raceways   (+44) 01283157935   www.raceways.co.uk
wheel stockists with huge range of
US wheels

Scootworks   (+1) 919269 0986   www.scootworks.com
suppliers of Phat Risers, handlebar risers
for bikes

Smart RRRs   (+44) 01904793232   www.smartrrrs.biz
custom seating of all types for trikes, bikes
and cars

Superbrace   (+1) 7148901830   www.superbrace.com
US company producing telescopic fork
braces

Taylormade   (+44) 01597860692   www.taylormade-wheels.co.uk
suppliers of custom wheels

Tow Pac   -   www.tow-pacinc.com
makes outrigger wheel kits for a large range
of bikes

Trike Covers bespoke trike covers	(+44) 01782744100	www.dbcovers.co.uk
Venhill high quality braking systems for bikes and trikes	(+44) 01306885111	www.venhill.co.uk
Weld aluminium racing wheels	(+1) 8007889325	www.weldracing.com
Zodiac performance products for cruisers, especially Harley-Davidson	dealers all over Europe	www.zodiac.nl

MOTORCYCLES SUITED TO TRIKE AND SIDECAR CONVERSION

BMW many BMW boxers are the basis of both trike and outfit conversions	–	www.bmw.co.uk
Harley-Davidson both the V-Rod and the classic V-twins have made ideal trikes	(+1) 4143434056	www.harley-davidson.com
Honda the GoldWing is the standard for big outfit and trike designs	(+44) 08452008000	www.honda.co.uk/motorcycles
Kawasaki the Vulcan V-twin has long been the basis of conversions	(+44) 08456002442	www.kawasaki.co.uk
Moto Guzzi once a favourite among chair pilots	–	www.motoguzzi.it
Neander not widely known yet, but may gain success as the first big diesel cruiser	–	www.neander-motors.com
Suzuki the Intruder cruisers make fine sidecar machines and at least one firm specialises in conversion to trikes	(+44) 08458508800	www.suzuki.co.uk
Triumph the Rocket III is considered th ultimate basis for three-wheel conversion, but the Thunderbird, Legend and Bonnie are also used	–	www.triumph.co.uk
Yamaha the DragStar & WildStar cruisers are a favourite basis for chair and trike work; the Midnight Star range may follow	–	www.yamaha-motor.co.uk

SOCIETIES

Brotherhood of the Third Wheel   -   www.btw-uk.co.uk
all trike fanciers

Federation of Sidecar Clubs   -   www.sidecars.org.uk
for all sidecar owners

**National Association of Bikers
with a Disability**   -   www.nabd.org.uk
all information available about conversions, grants and rallies

Two distinctive alternatives. Above a Suzuki TL1000S / Merlin outfit (photo courtesy Merlin Sidecars) and below, a Boss Hoss Sierra (photo courtesy Boss Hoss Cycles)